WISE PUBLICATIONS
part of The Music Sales Group
London / New York / Paris / Sydney / Copenhagen /
Berlin / Madrid / Hong Kong / Tokyo

Published by
Wise Publications
14-15 Berners Street, London W1T 3LJ, UK.

Exclusive Distributors:

Music Sales Limited
Distribution Centre, Newmarket Road,
Bury St Edmunds, Suffolk IP33 3YB, UK.

Music Sales Pty Limited
4th floor, Lisgar House, 30-32 Carrington Street,
Sydney, NSW 2000, Australia.

Order No. AM1011241
ISBN: 978-1-78558-185-4
Wise Publications,
a division of Music Sales Limited.

Compiled and edited by Jenni Norey.
Cover design by Tim Field.
Printed in the EU.

The Grand Staff

Music for the piano or keyboard is usually written on a **grand staff** — two staves joined by a **brace**.

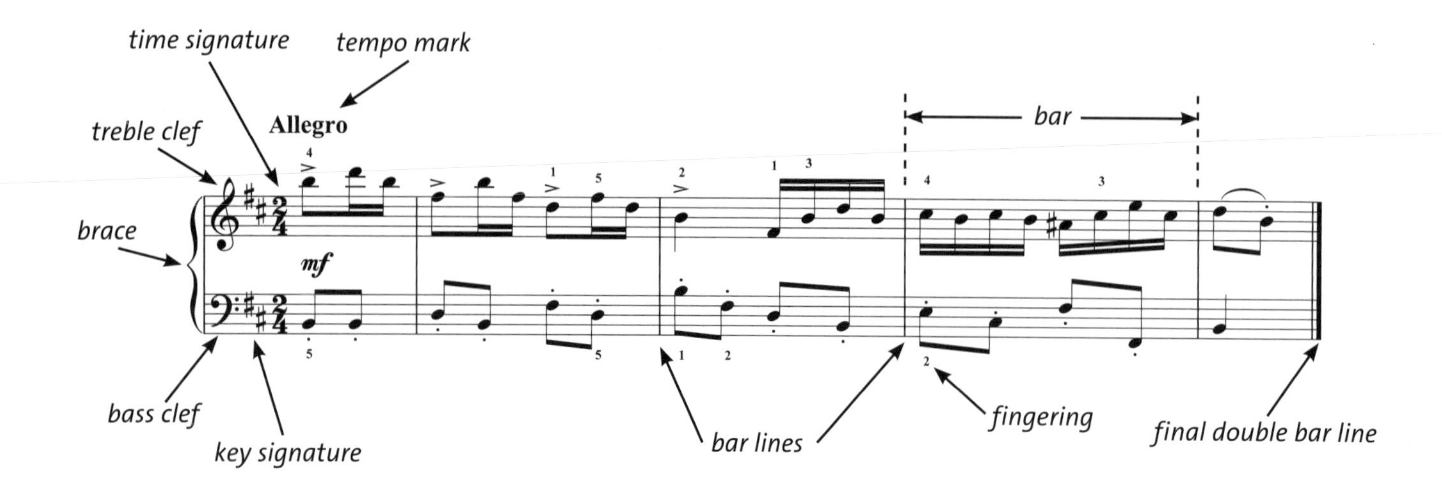

Notes on the upper stave, headed by the **treble clef** (or *G clef*), are usually played by the right hand.

Notes on the lower stave, headed by the **bass clef** (or *F clef*), are usually played by the left hand.

The music is divided by **bar lines** into **bars**. Usually, each bar contains the same number of beats (counts), as indicated by the **time signature** at the beginning of the music.

Notes values and rests

The note value tells you the duration of a note — how many beats it lasts. When read in sequence, note values show the rhythm of the music.

Each has its own rest, which indicates a silence for the equivalent duration.

symbol	*name*	*duration*	*rest*
𝅝	semibreve	4 beats	𝄻
𝅗𝅥 or 𝅗𝅥	minim	2 beats	𝄼
♩ or ♩	crotchet	1 beat	𝄽
♪ or ♪	quaver	½ beat	𝄾
𝅘𝅥𝅯 or 𝅘𝅥𝅯	semiquaver	¼ beat	𝄿

Clefs

𝄞 The right hand usually plays music written in the **treble clef**.

This is also called the *G clef* because it spirals around the line on which the note G above Middle C is written.

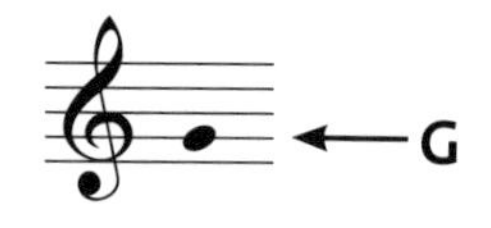

𝄢 The left hand usually plays music written in the **bass clef**.

This is also called the *F clef* because there are two dots either side of the line on which the note F below Middle C is written.

Sharps, flats and naturals

♯ A **sharp** sign raises the pitch of a note by a semitone to the very next key on the right.

♭ A **flat** sign lowers the pitch of a note by a semitone to the very next key on the left.

♮ A **natural** sign cancels the effect of a sharp or a flat, representing the unaltered pitch.

A **key signature** is written at the start of each line of music. It tells us which notes should be played as *sharps* or *flats* and saves writing a ♯ or ♭ sign every time these notes appear.

Time signatures

The **time signature** appears after the key signature at the beginning of the music.

The *upper figure* shows the number of beats in each bar and the *lower figure* tells us what note duration gets one beat.

4/4 *or* C = four crotchet beats per bar *(also called common time)*

3/4 = three crotchet beats per bar

2/4 = two crotchet beats per bar

2/2 *or* ¢ = two minim beats per bar *(also called cut common time)*

6/8 = six quaver beats per bar

12/8 = twelve quaver beats per bar

Other musical signs

A **double bar line** marks the beginning of a new section of music.

A **final double bar line** marks the end of a piece.

A **slur** is a curved line, over or under a group of notes, indicating that they should be played smoothly (*legato*).

A **tie** is a curved line, connecting two consecutive notes of the same pitch — only the first should be played and then held for the combined value of both notes.

A **staccato** dot, above or below a note, indicates that the note should be played as short and detached.

An **accent** mark, above or below a note, indicates that it should be emphasized by playing it louder than the general dynamic.

A **fermata** (or **pause**) indicates that the note should be held for longer than its written duration.

Fingering numbers

Your fingers are given numbers from 1 to 5, starting with the thumbs and numbering outwards.

Fingering is sometimes written above or below notes to help you move your hands around the keyboard efficiently.

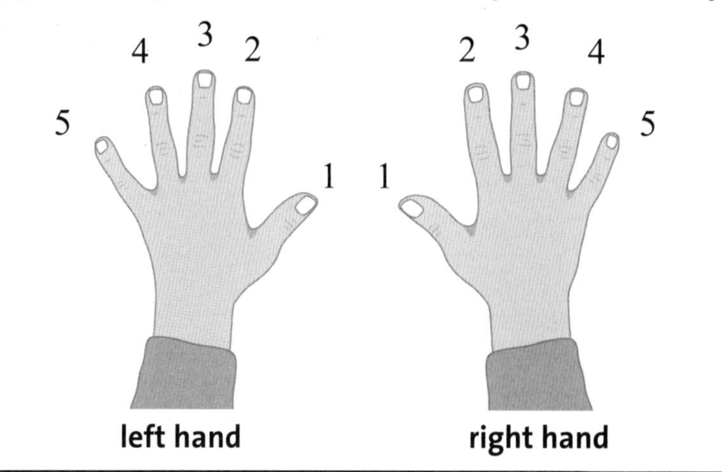

Dynamics

A **dynamic mark** tells you how loudly or softly to play.

pp	**pianissimo**	very soft
p	**piano**	soft
mp	**mezzo piano**	moderately soft
mf	**mezzo forte**	moderately loud
f	**forte**	loud
ff	**fortissimo**	very loud
<	**crescendo** *cresc.*	gradually getting louder
>	**diminuendo** *dim.*	gradually getting softer

Repeat signs and other navigation marks

:‖ This is an end **repeat sign**, which tells you to repeat back from the beginning, or from the start repeat: ‖:

1. 2. **First-** and **second-time bars** are used to indicate passages in a repeated section that are only performed on certain playings.

D.C. *(Da Capo)* tells you to repeat from the beginning.

D.C. al Fine *(Da Capo al Fine)* tells you to repeat from the beginning to the end, or up to **Fine**.

D.S. *(Dal Segno)* tells you to repeat from the sign 𝄋.

D.S. al Coda *(Dal Segno al Coda)* tells you to repeat from the sign 𝄋 and then, when you reach **to Coda** 𝄌, you should jump to the Coda, marked 𝄌 **Coda**.

Key signatures

The key of the music is indicated by the **key signature** at the start of each stave, just after the clef. It tells you which notes in the music should be played as *sharps* or *flats*.

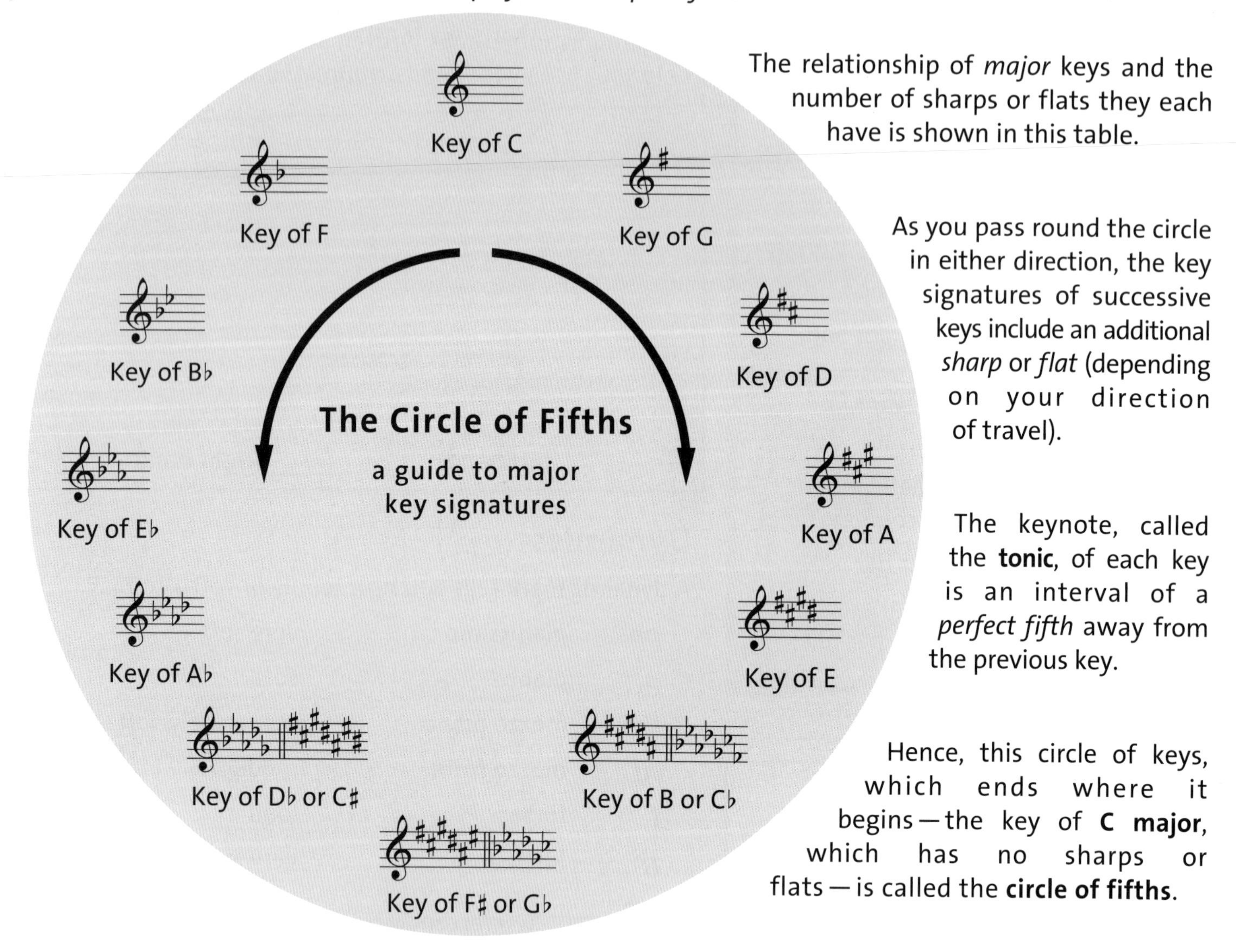

The relationship of *major* keys and the number of sharps or flats they each have is shown in this table.

As you pass round the circle in either direction, the key signatures of successive keys include an additional *sharp* or *flat* (depending on your direction of travel).

The keynote, called the **tonic**, of each key is an interval of a *perfect fifth* away from the previous key.

Hence, this circle of keys, which ends where it begins — the key of **C major**, which has no sharps or flats — is called the **circle of fifths**.

More about note values and rhythms

A **dotted note** lasts for 1½ times its usual duration.

symbol	*name*	*duration*	*rest*
𝅗𝅥. *or* 𝅗𝅥.	dotted minim	3 beats	𝄼.
♩. *or* ♩.	dotted crotchet	1½ beats	𝄽.
♪. *or* ♪.	dotted quaver	¾ beat	𝄾.

A **triplet** is a subdivision of a beat or beats into three notes of equal duration. Using any note value as a unit, three *triplet* notes divide the duration that two notes would normally occupy into three.

Triplet quavers (3 ♪♪♪) *divide a crotchet (two quavers) into three*

Triplet crotchets (3 ♩♩♩) *divide a minim (two crotchets) into three*

A **beam** is often used to join note values of a *quaver* or shorter to show a rhythmic grouping.

The most common grouping is by *crotchet* beat, which can help you see where the beats of the bar fall.

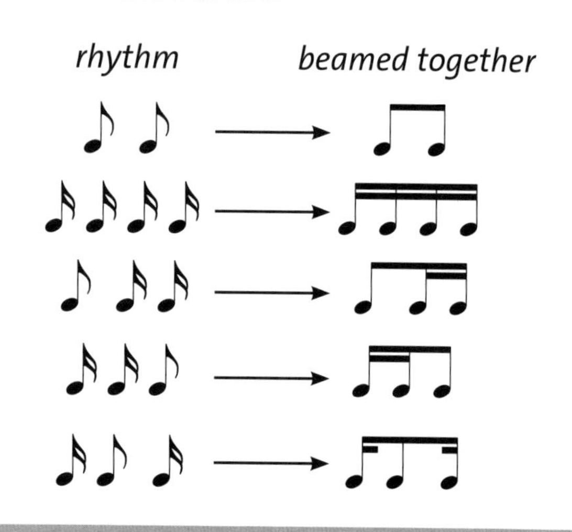

Intervals and chords

An **interval** is the distance in pitch between two notes. They are measured and named according to the number of degrees of the scale they comprise. When two notes are played consecutively they form a *melodic interval*, and when they are sounded together, they form a *harmonic interval*.

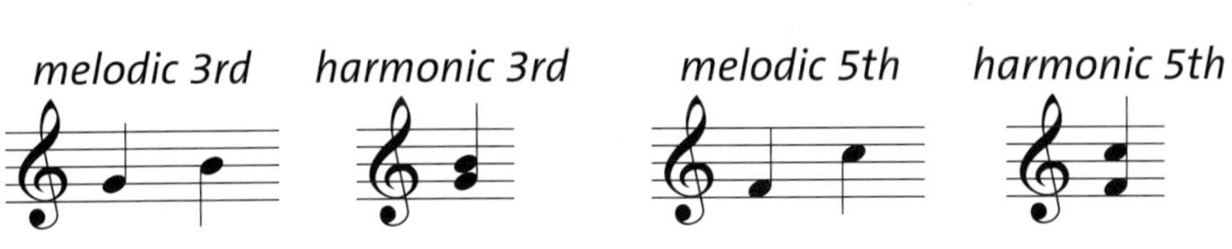

A **chord** consists of two or more tones sounded together. A **tonic triad** is a chord comprising three degrees of the scale: *tonic*, *3rd* and *5th*.

Common major and minor chords

Major tonic triads

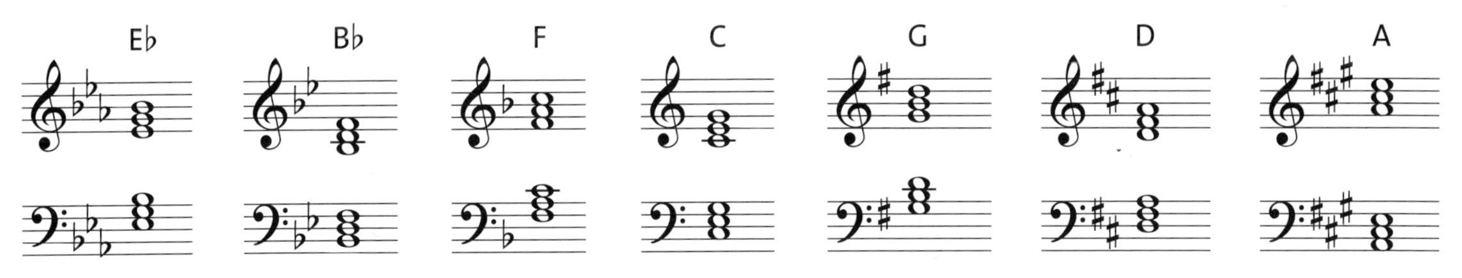

Minor tonic triads

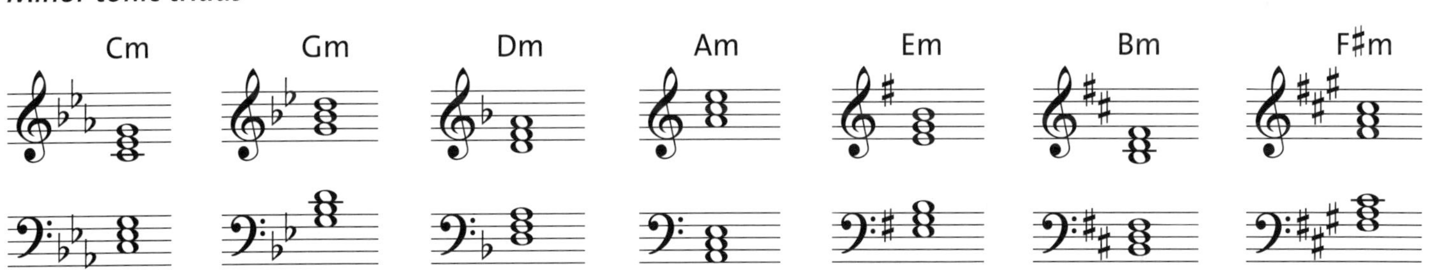

Tempo marks

A **tempo mark** at the start of a passage of music tells you what speed to play at. They are often written in Italian.

Steady tempo

slow	**Grave**	very slowly, dragging
	Largo	broadly
	Lento	slowly
	Adagio	slowly, stately
	Andante	at a walking pace
	Moderato	moderately
	Allegro	fast, brightly
	Vivace	lively
	Presto	very fast
fast	**Prestissimo**	faster than Presto

A change of tempo

ritardando (rit.)	gradually getting slower
rallentando (rall.)	gradually getting slower
poco rit.	getting a little slower
allargando	getting broader, slowing
meno mosso	less movement, slower
accelerando (accel.)	gradually getting faster
più mosso	more movement, faster
a tempo	resume original tempo

Metronome marks

A **metronome mark** may be written at the start of the music to show the precise speed at which it should be played, for example, ♩ = 72 tells you that there are 72 crotchet beats per minute.

Note Guide

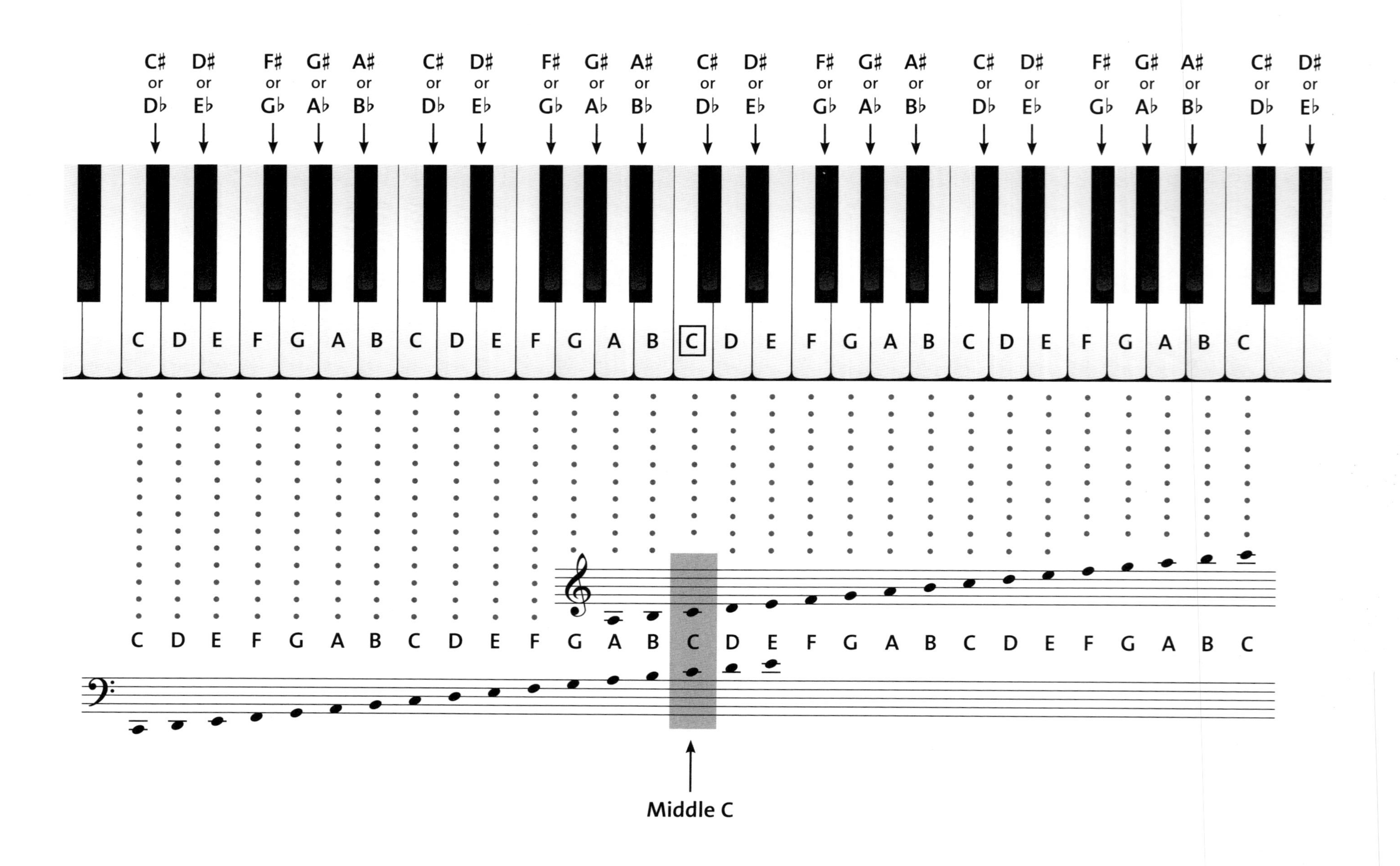
C♯ or D♭ D♯ or E♭ F♯ or G♭ G♯ or A♭ A♯ or B♭ C♯ or D♭ D♯ or E♭ F♯ or G♭ G♯ or A♭ A♯ or B♭ C♯ or D♭ D♯ or E♭ F♯ or G♭ G♯ or A♭ A♯ or B♭ C♯ or D♭ D♯ or E♭ F♯ or G♭ G♯ or A♭ A♯ or B♭ C♯ or D♭ D♯ or E♭
C D E F G A B C D E F G A B C D E F G A B C D E F G A B C
C D E F G A B C D E F G A B C D E F G A B C D E F G A B C
Middle C

Are You With Me

Words & Music by Tommy James, Terry McBride
& Shane McAnally

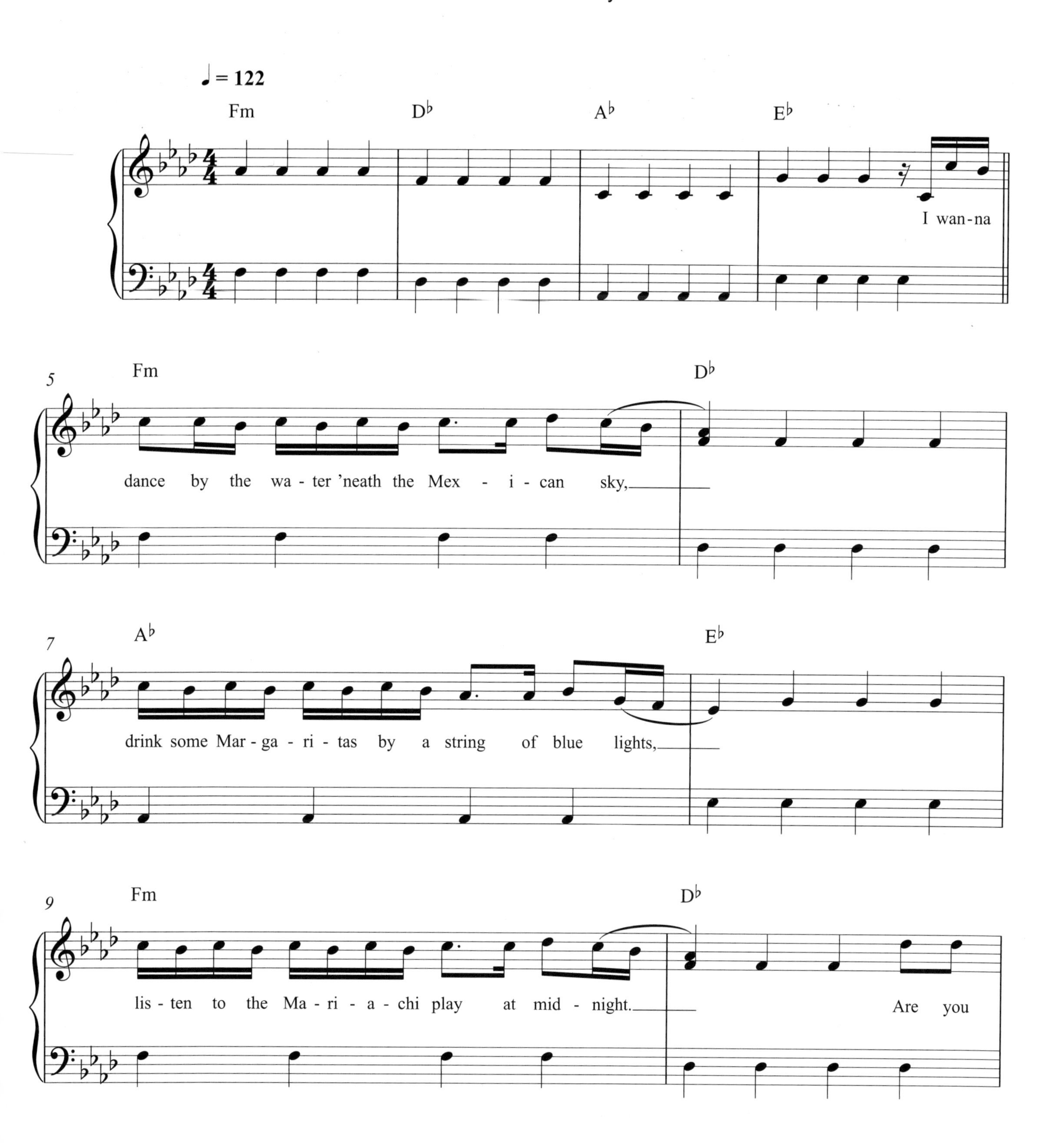

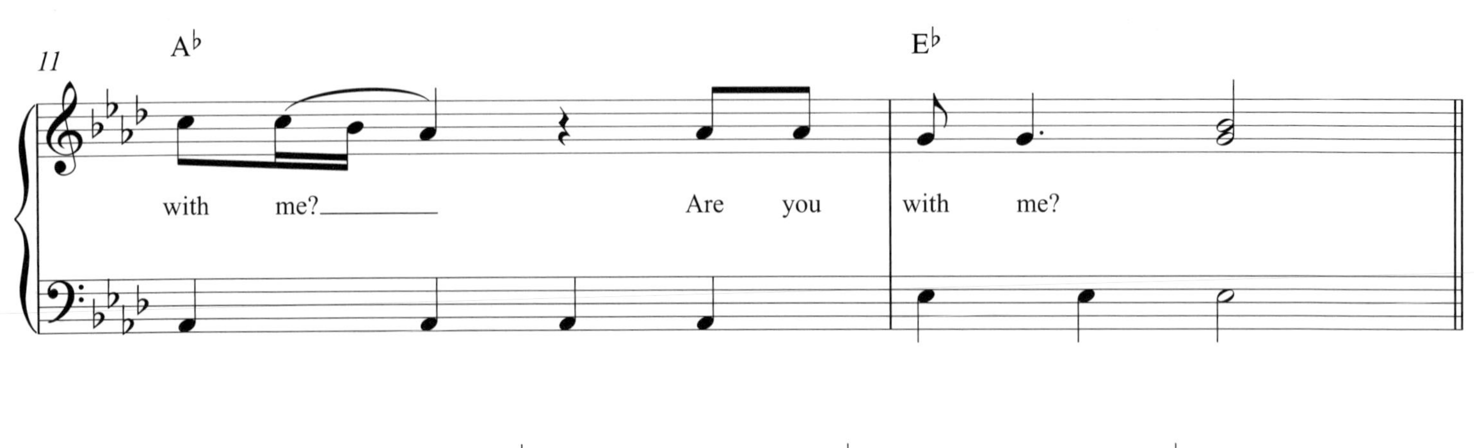
11
A♭
E♭
with me?
Are you
with me?

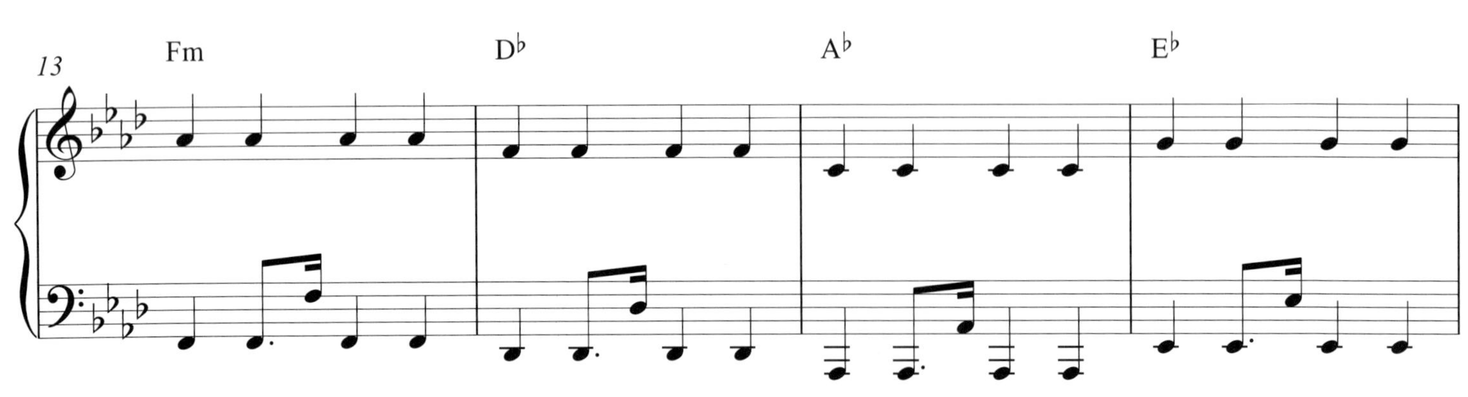
13
Fm
D♭
A♭
E♭

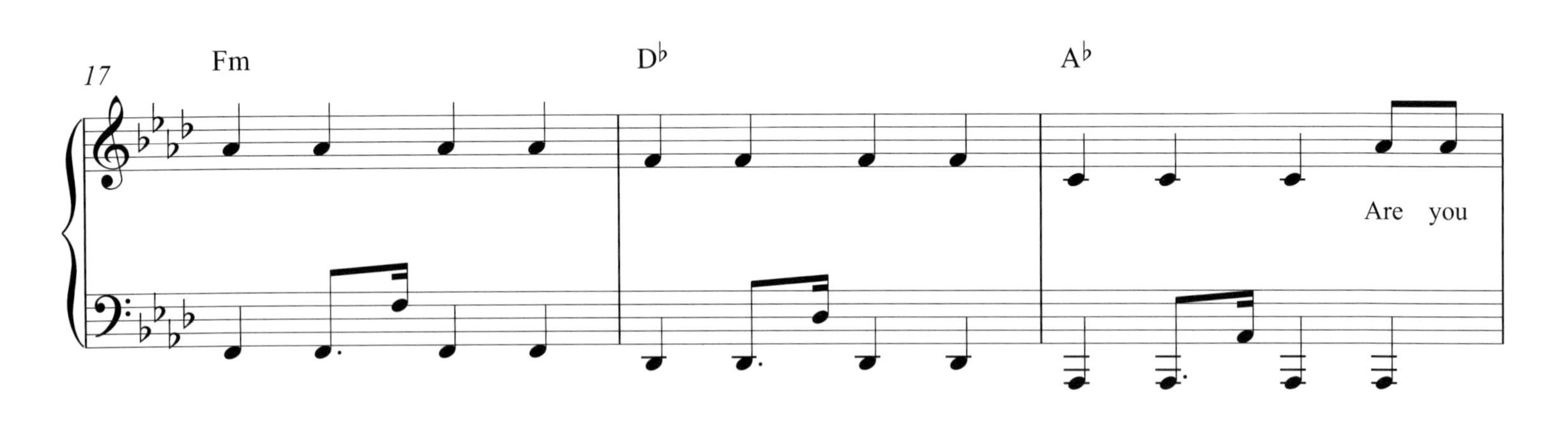
17
Fm
D♭
A♭
Are you

20
E♭
Fm
D♭
with me?

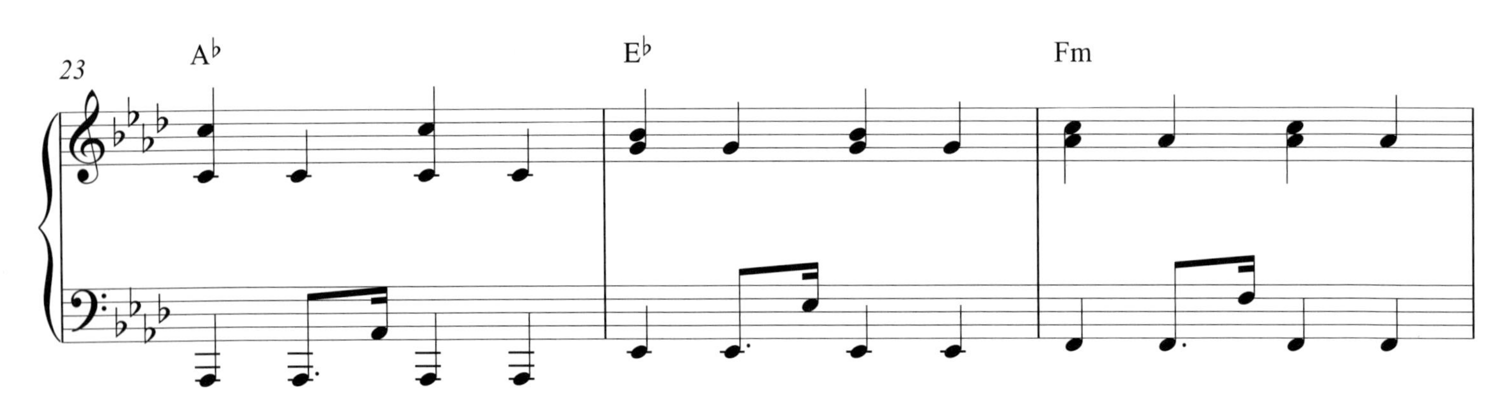
23
A♭
E♭
Fm

26
D♭
A♭
E♭
Are you
with me?
29
Fm
D♭
A♭
32
E♭
Fm
(Lis - ten to the Ma - ri - a - chi play at mid - night.)
34
D♭
A♭
E♭
Are you
with me?
Are you
with me?
I wan-na
37
Fm
D♭
dance by the wa - ter 'neath the Mex - i - can sky,

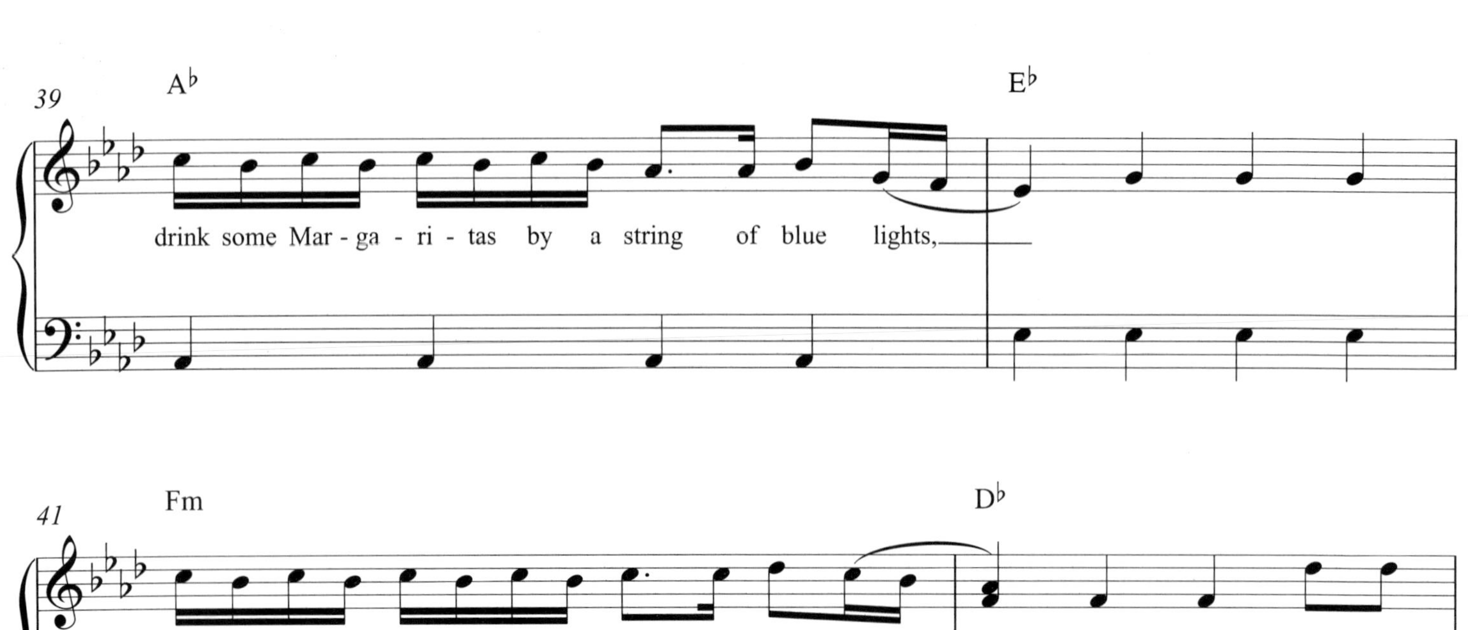
39
A♭
E♭
drink some Mar - ga - ri - tas by a string of blue lights,

41
Fm
D♭
lis - ten to the Ma - ri - a - chi play at mid - night.
Are you

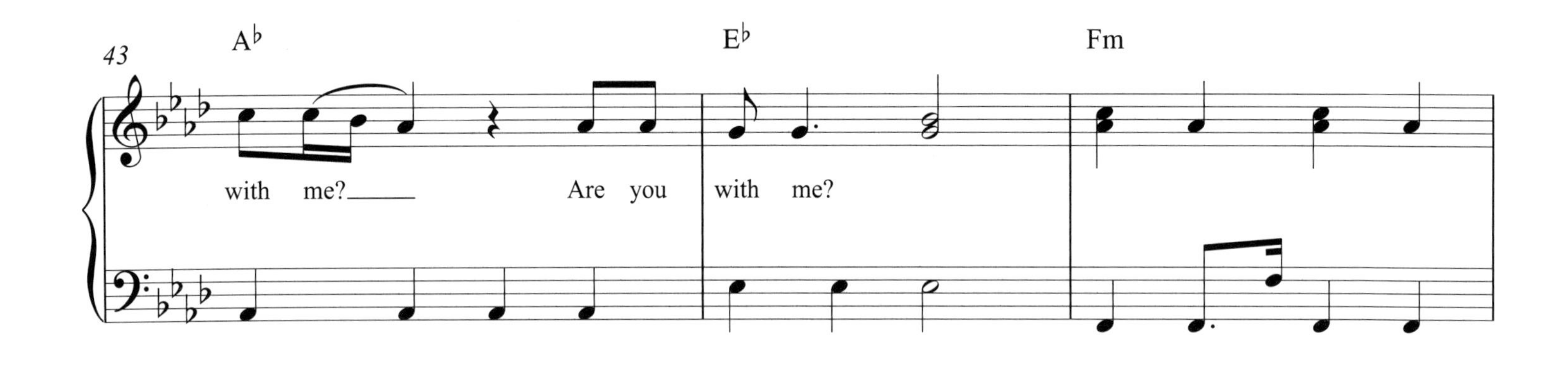
43
A♭
E♭
Fm
with me?
Are you
with me?

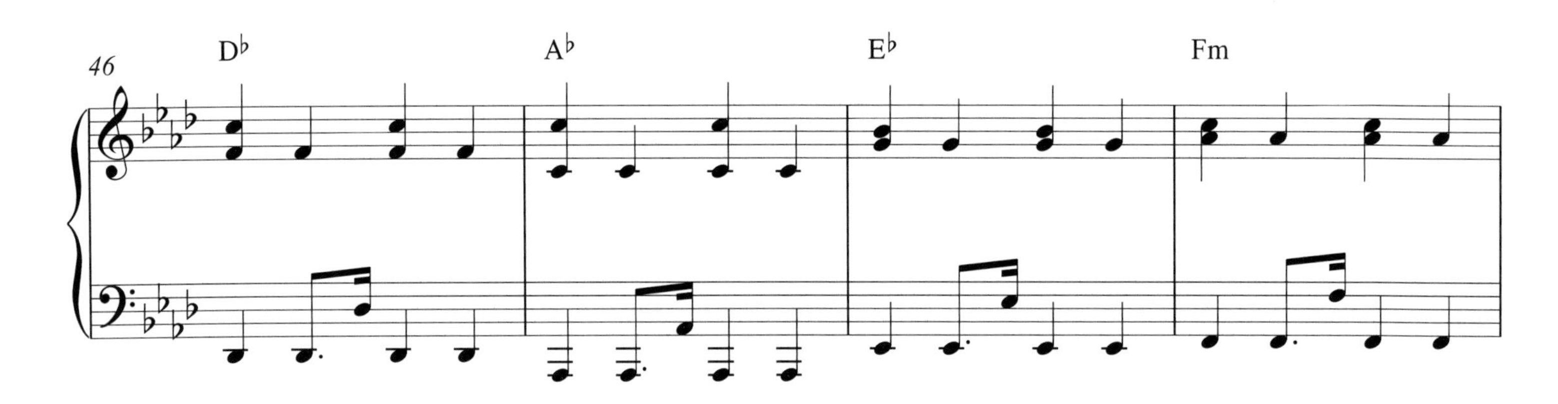
46
D♭
A♭
E♭
Fm

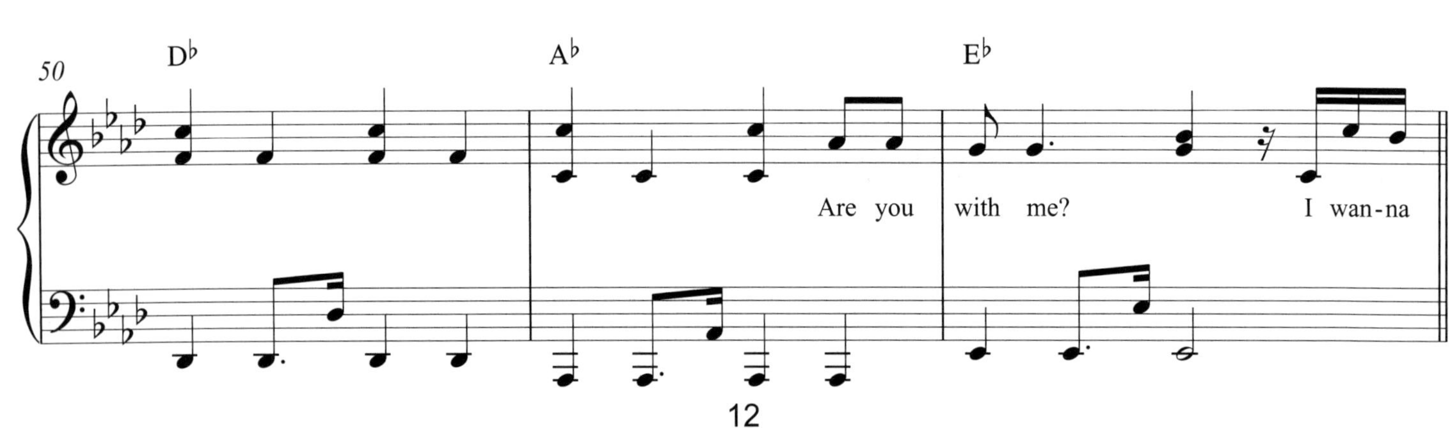
50
D♭
A♭
E♭
Are you
with me?
I wan-na

53
Fm
D♭
dance by the wa - ter 'neath the Mex - i - can sky,

55
A♭
E♭
drink some Mar - ga - ri - tas by a string of blue lights,

57
Fm
D♭
lis - ten to the Ma - ri - a - chi play at mid - night. Are you

59
A♭
1.
E♭
2.
E♭
with me? Are you with me? I wan-na with me?

Bills

Words & Music by Jacob Hindlin, Eric Frederic,
Rickard Goransson & Gamal Lewis

15
C7sus4
F
C7sus4
To Coda
F
make sure ev - 'ry - bod - y eats. I got bills! 1. All these bills pil - ing up on my
2. Woke up and I bumped my head,
18
desk, they look - in' like a moun - tain. All you lit - tle kids run - ning 'round, I could
stubbed my toe on the edge of the bed. O - pened the fridge, and the food all gone,
20
C7
F
hear their sto - machs growl - in'. There's a full moon out, and my
neigh - bour damn dog done crapped on my lawn. Hopped in the car and the car won't start, it's
22
girl just keep on howl - in'. Says she's gon - na leave me if I don't come
too damn hot, but I still got - ta walk. Be - hind an old la - dy in the gro - ce - ry line,
24
C7
G♭9
C7sus4
home with fif - ty thou - sand. God
pray - ing that my card don't get de - clined.

26
F
B♭
G♭9
C7sus4
damn, God damn, God damn, God damn.
Oh
28
F
B♭
G♭9
C7sus4
man, oh man, oh man, oh man.
God
30
F
B♭
G♭9
C7sus4
D.S. al Coda
damn, oh man, God damn, oh man.
I got
Coda
33
F
B♭
A
Dm
35
C7sus4
F
C7sus4

37
G♭9
C7sus4
F
B♭
G♭9
C7sus4
And my
shoes,
my shoes,
40
F
B♭
G♭9
C7sus4
F
B♭
I said my
shoes
ain't got no
43
G♭9
G7/B
C7sus4
N.C.
soles.
I got
47
F
B♭
A
Dm
C7sus4
F
bills
I got - ta
pay
so I'm gon'
work, work, work ev - 'ry
50
C7sus4
F
B♭
A
Dm
day
I got
mouths
I got - ta
feed,
so I'm gon'

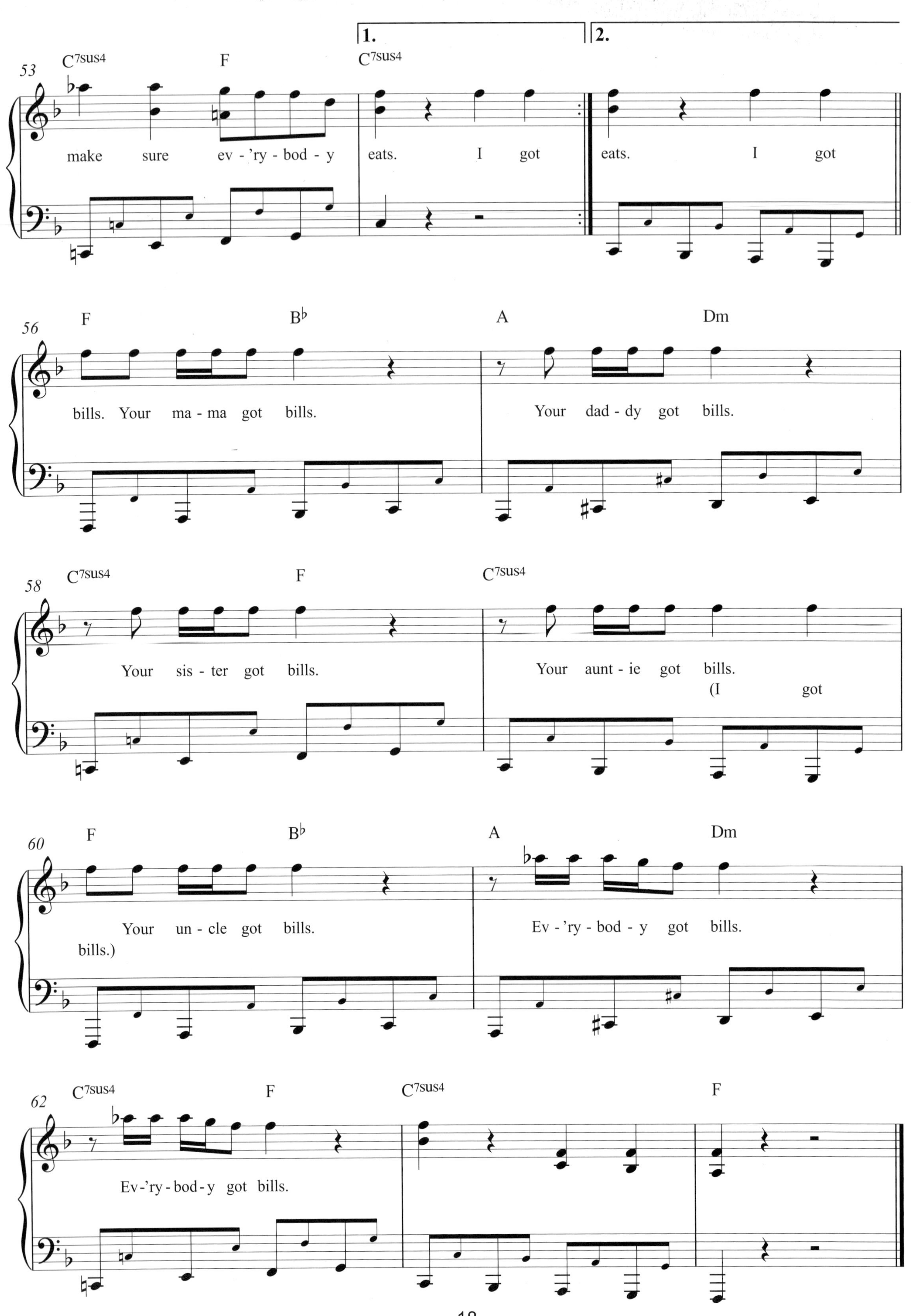
1.
2.
53
C7sus4
F
C7sus4
make sure ev - 'ry - bod - y eats. I got
eats. I got
56
F
B♭
A
Dm
bills. Your ma - ma got bills. Your dad - dy got bills.
58
C7sus4
F
C7sus4
Your sis - ter got bills. Your aunt - ie got bills.
(I got
60
F
B♭
A
Dm
Your un - cle got bills. Ev - 'ry - bod - y got bills.
bills.)
62
C7sus4
F
C7sus4
F
Ev-'ry-bod-y got bills.

Black Magic

Words & Music by Edvard Erfjord, Henrik Michelsen,
Camille Purcell & Edward Drewett

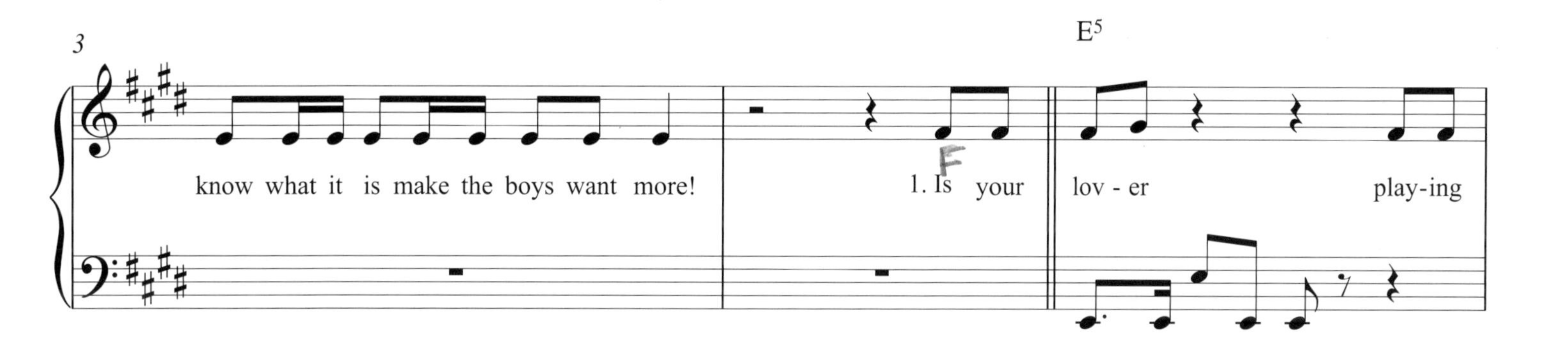

13
E5
honey, just to make him sweet. Crystal balling, just to
(2.) lookin' for Mister Right. Need that magic to change him
16
A5
help him see what he's been missing. So come and get it while you've still got time.
over night. Here's the answer, come and get it while you've still got time.
19
E5
C♯m
Get your boy on his knees and repeat after me,
22
B
E
say: "Take a sip of my secret potion, I'll make you fall in love.
25
Amaj7
For a spell that can't be broken, one drop should be enough.

27
C♯m
Boy, you be - long to me,
B
I got the rec - i - pe and it's
29
A
called Black Ma - gic." (And it's called Black Ma - gic.)
31
E
"Take a sip of my se-cret po-tion, one taste and you'll be mine.
Amaj7
It's a spell that can't be bro-ken,
34
it-'ll keep you up all night.
C♯m
Boy, you be-long to me,
B
I got the rec - i - pe and it's
37
A
To Coda
1.
2.
called Black Ma - gic." (And it's called Black Ma - gic.) 2.If you're called Black Ma - gic.) All the

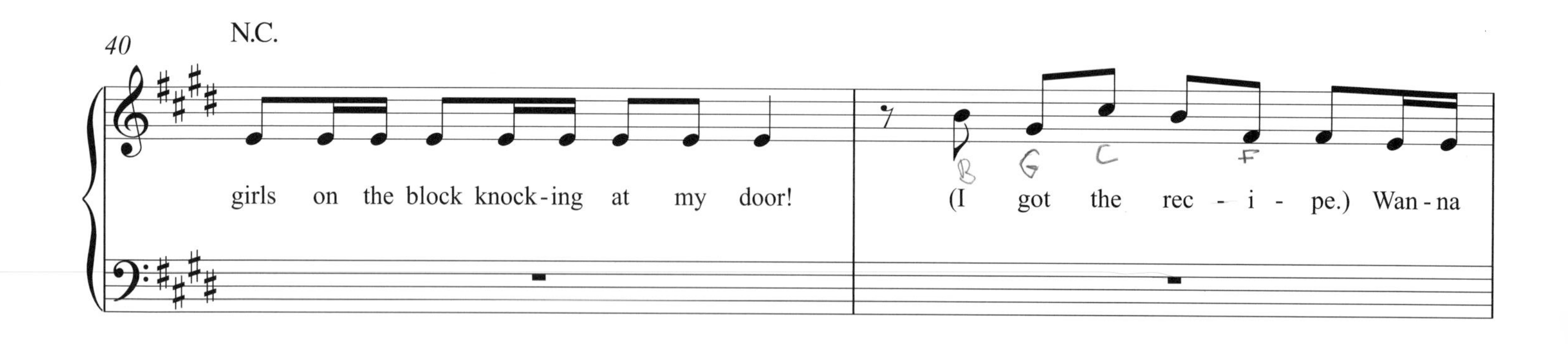
40
N.C.
girls on the block knock-ing at my door!
(I got the rec - i - pe.) Wan-na

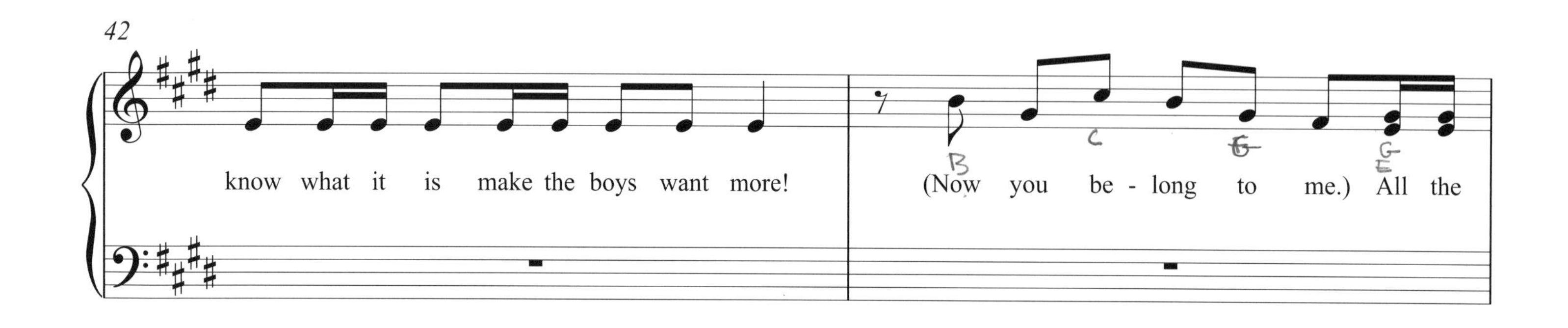
42
know what it is make the boys want more!
(Now you be - long to me.) All the

44
E
N.C.
girls on the block knock-ing at my door!
(I got the rec - i - pe.) Wan-na

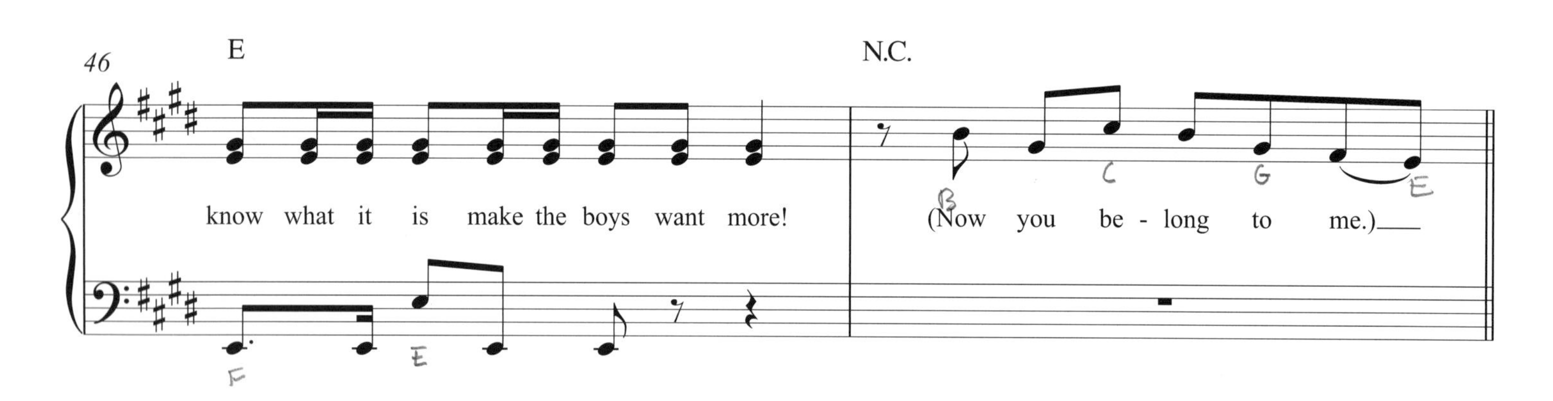
46
E
N.C.
know what it is make the boys want more!
(Now you be - long to me.)

48
E
Amaj7
Take a sip of my se-cret po-tion,
I'll make you fall in love.
For a spell that can't be bro-ken,

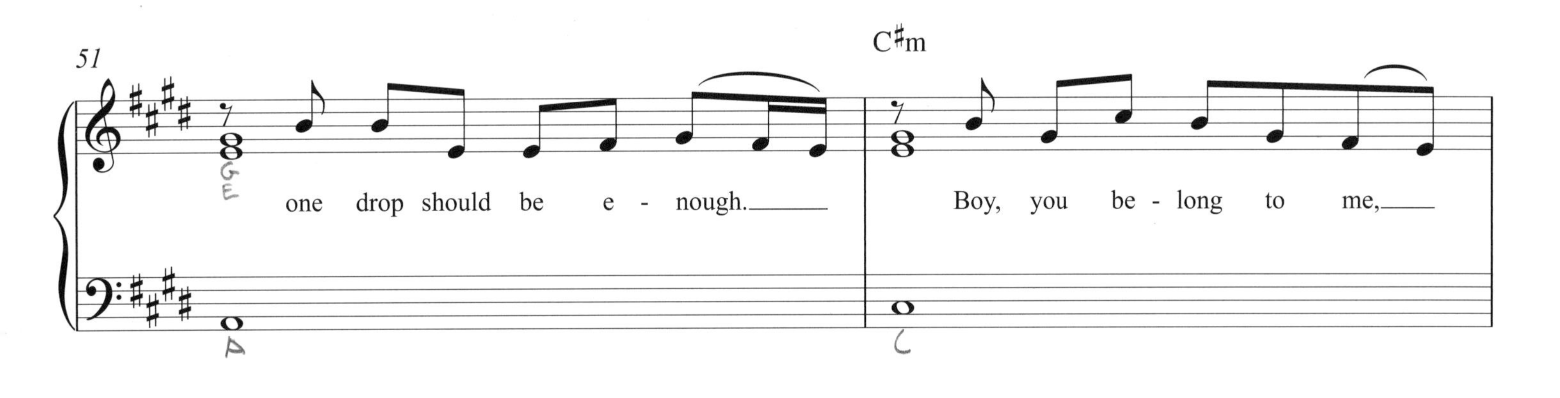
51
C♯m
one drop should be e - nough.
Boy, you be - long to me,
G
E
A
C

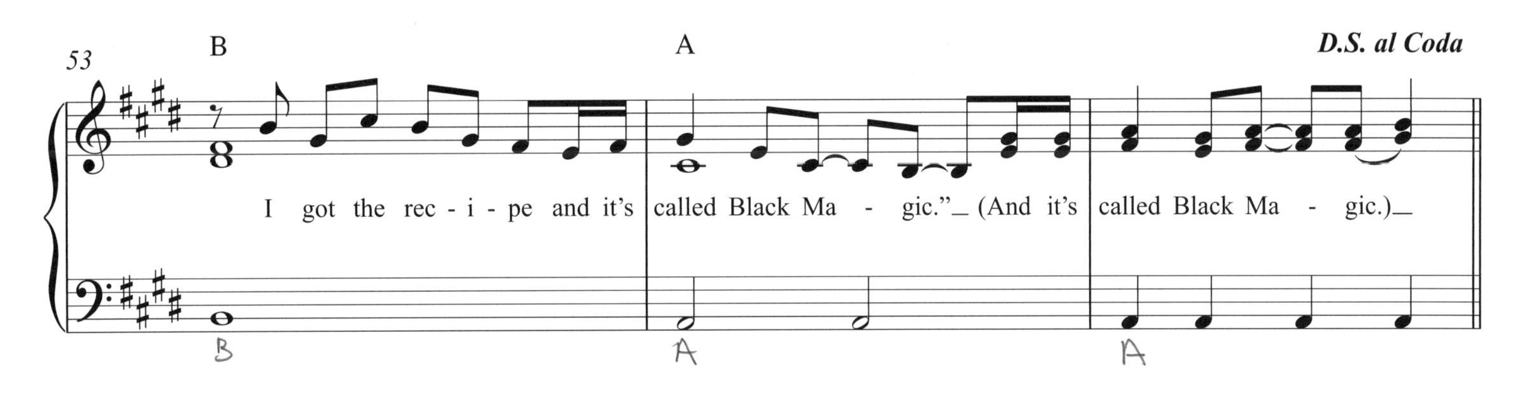
53
B
A
D.S. al Coda
I got the rec - i - pe and it's called Black Ma - gic." (And it's called Black Ma - gic.)
B
A
A

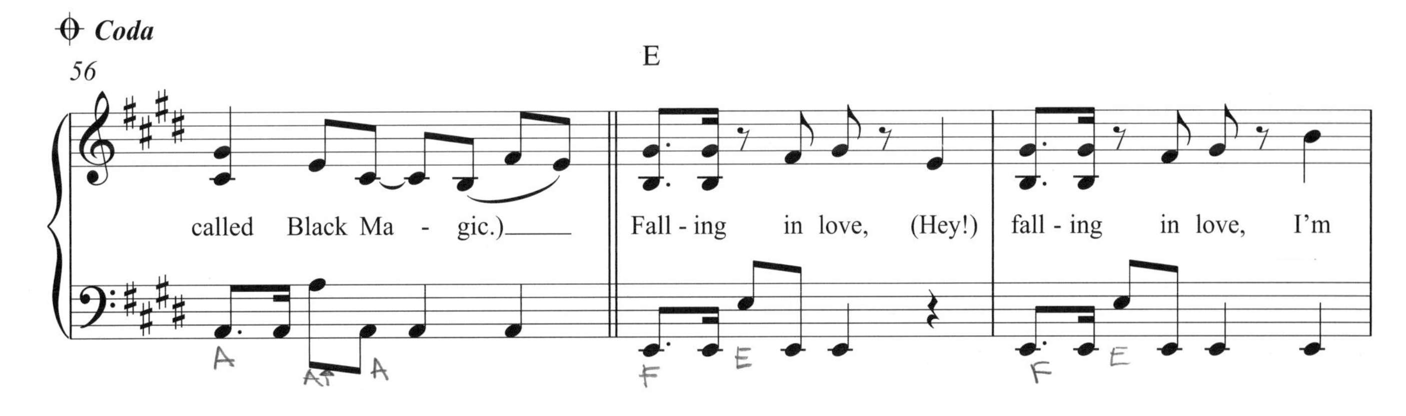
Coda
56
E
called Black Ma - gic.)
Fall - ing in love, (Hey!) fall - ing in love, I'm

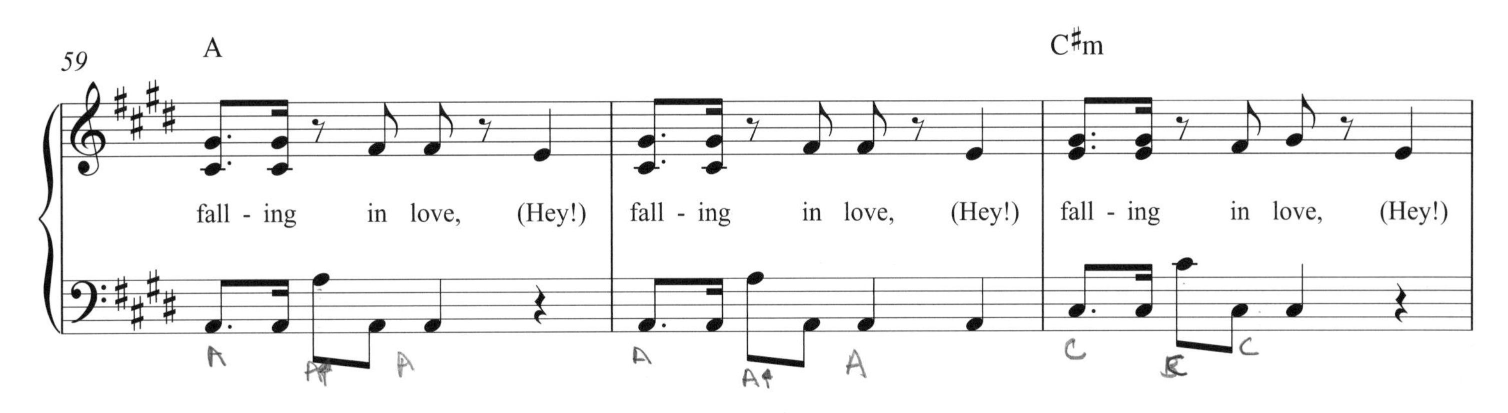
59
A
C♯m
fall - ing in love, (Hey!) fall - ing in love, (Hey!) fall - ing in love, (Hey!)

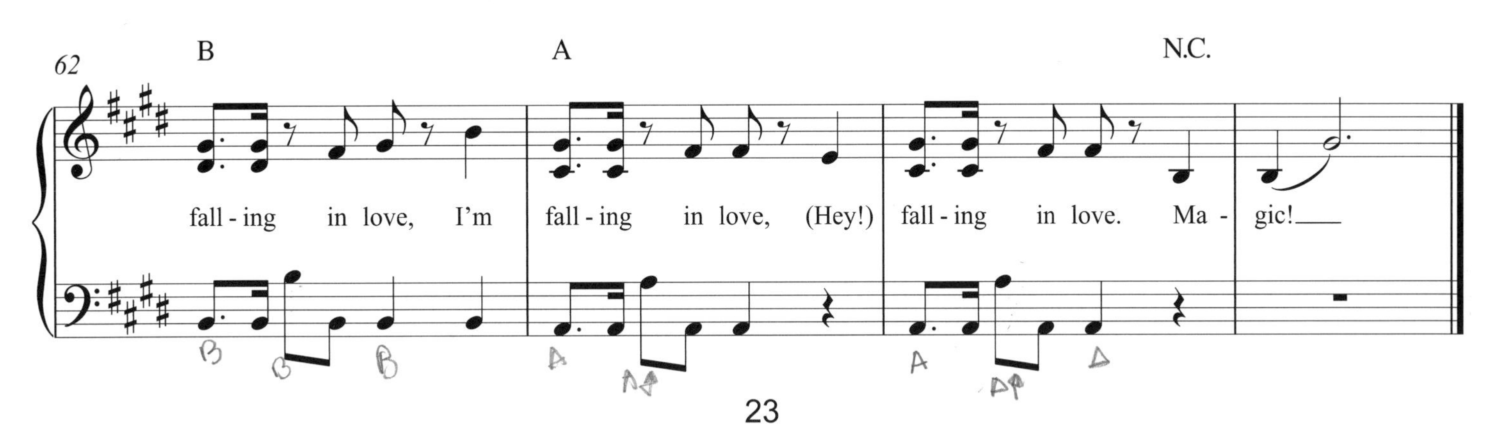
62
B
A
N.C.
fall - ing in love, I'm fall - ing in love, (Hey!) fall - ing in love. Ma - gic!

Blame It On Me

Words & Music by Joel Pott & George Ezra Barnett

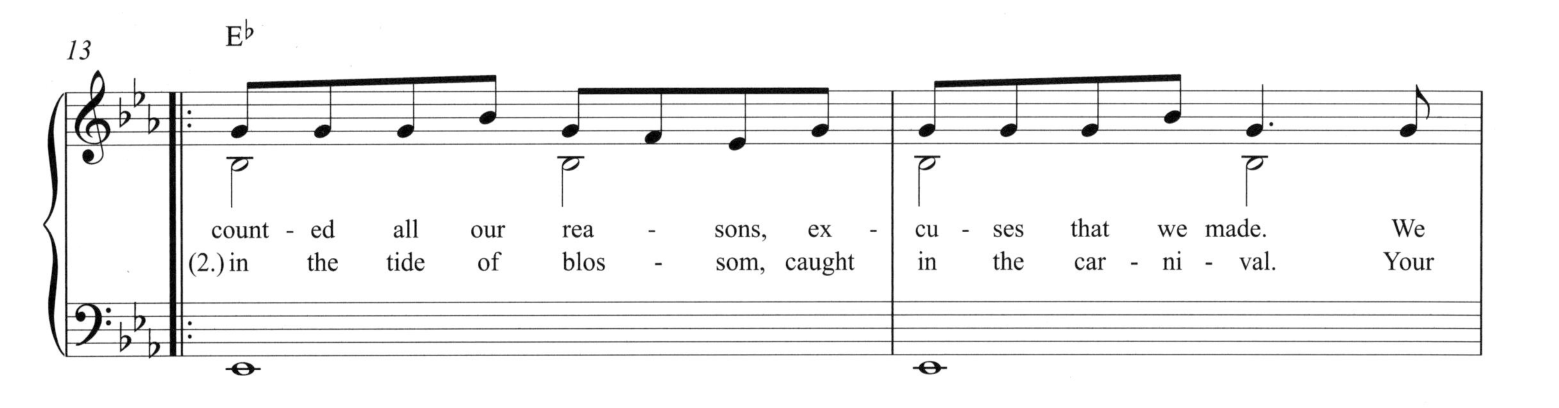
13
E♭
count - ed all our rea - sons, ex - cu - ses that we made. We
(2.) in the tide of blos - som, caught in the car - ni - val. Your

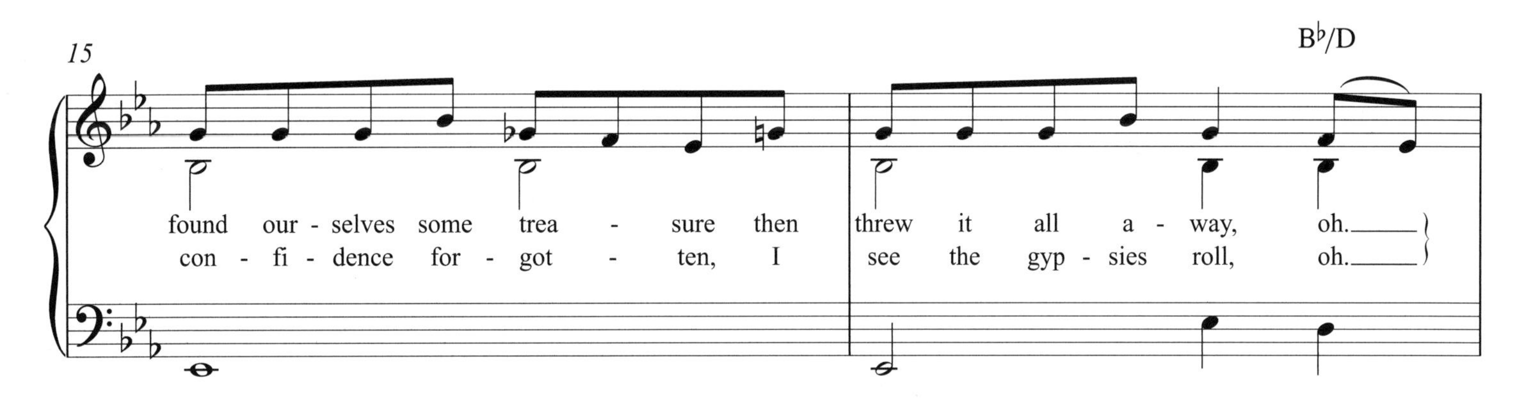
15
B♭/D
found our - selves some trea - sure then threw it all a - way, oh.
con - fi - dence for - got - ten, I see the gyp - sies roll, oh.

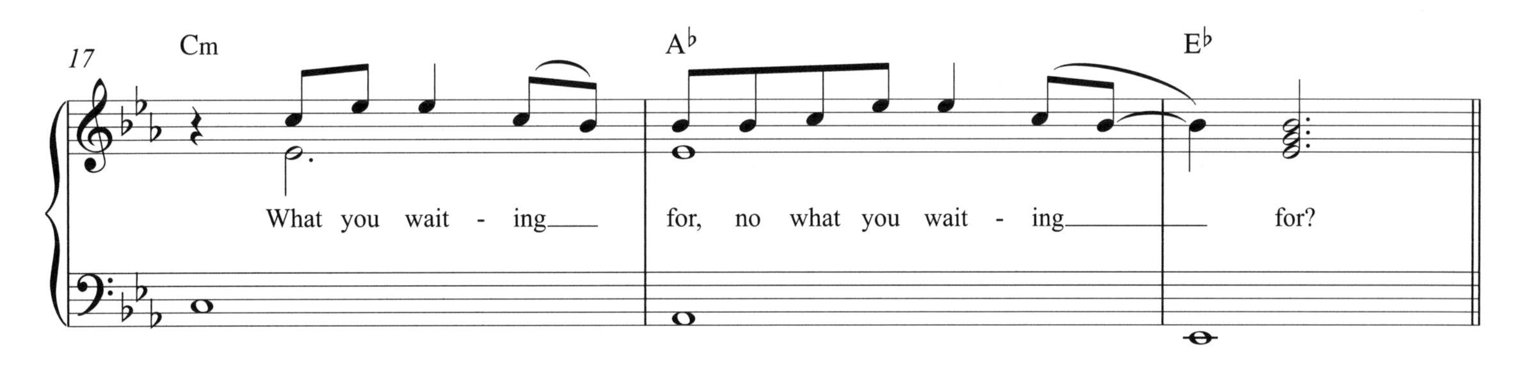
17
Cm
A♭
E♭
What you wait - ing for, no what you wait - ing for?

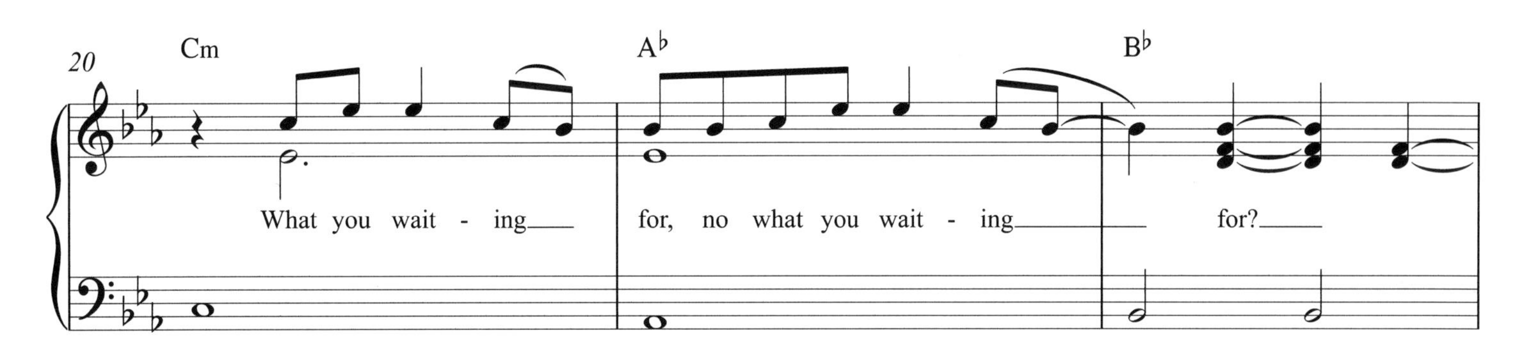
20
Cm
A♭
B♭
What you wait - ing for, no what you wait - ing for?

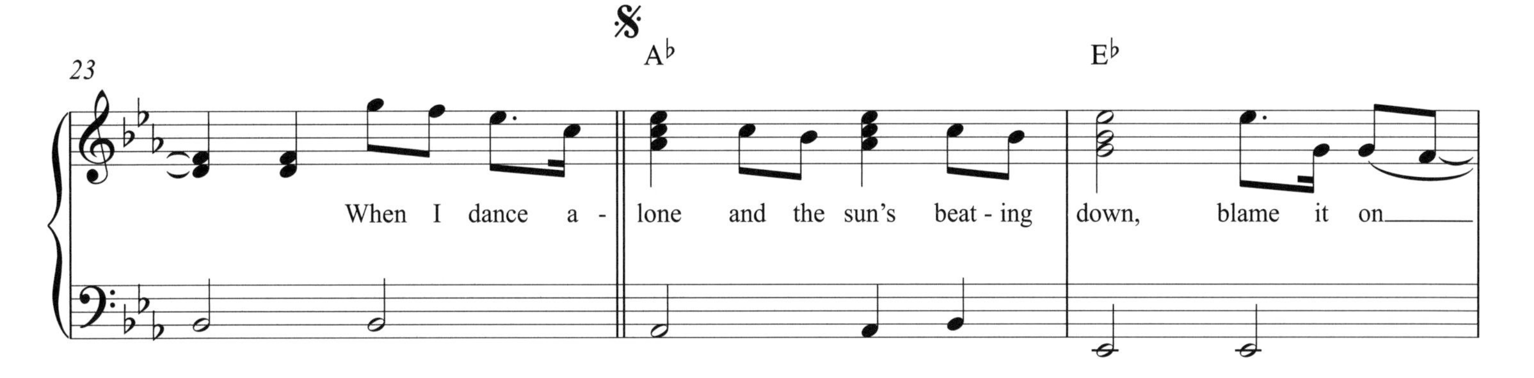
23
A♭
E♭
When I dance a - lone and the sun's beat - ing down, blame it on

26
B♭
A♭
me.
When I lose con - trol and the veil's o - ver -
29
E♭
B♭
To Coda
Cm
1.
-used blame it on me.
What you wait - ing
32
A♭
E♭
A♭/E♭
E♭
A♭/E♭
for, no what you wait - ing for?
2. Caught
2.
35
B♭
Cm
A♭
E♭
What you wait - ing for, no what you wait - ing for?
39
Cm
A♭
B♭
D.S. al Coda
What you wait - ing for, no what you wait - ing for?
When I dance a -

Coda
43
B♭
A♭
When I dance a - lone, I know I'll
45
E♭
B♭
go, blame it on me, oh. When I lose con -

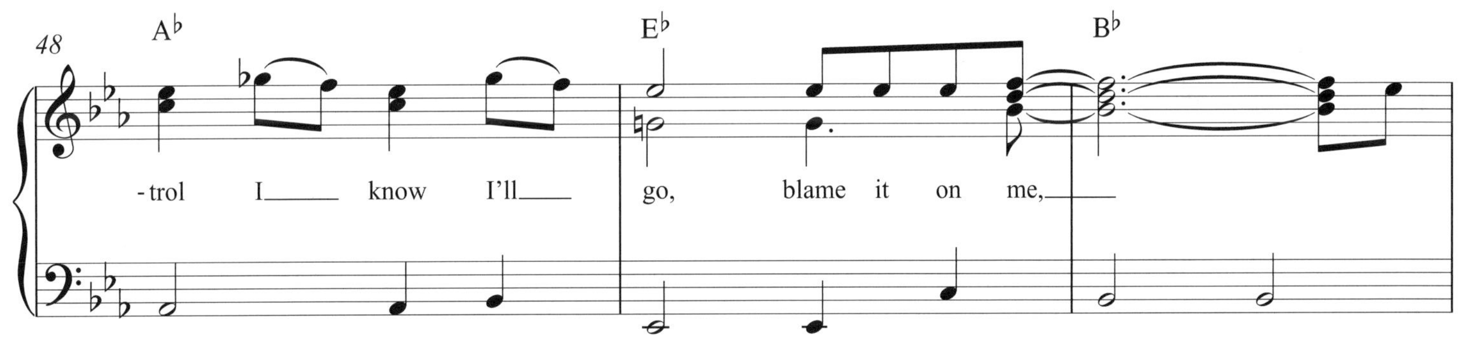
48
A♭
E♭
B♭
-trol I know I'll go, blame it on me,

51
Cm
A♭
oh. What you wait - ing for, no what you wait - ing

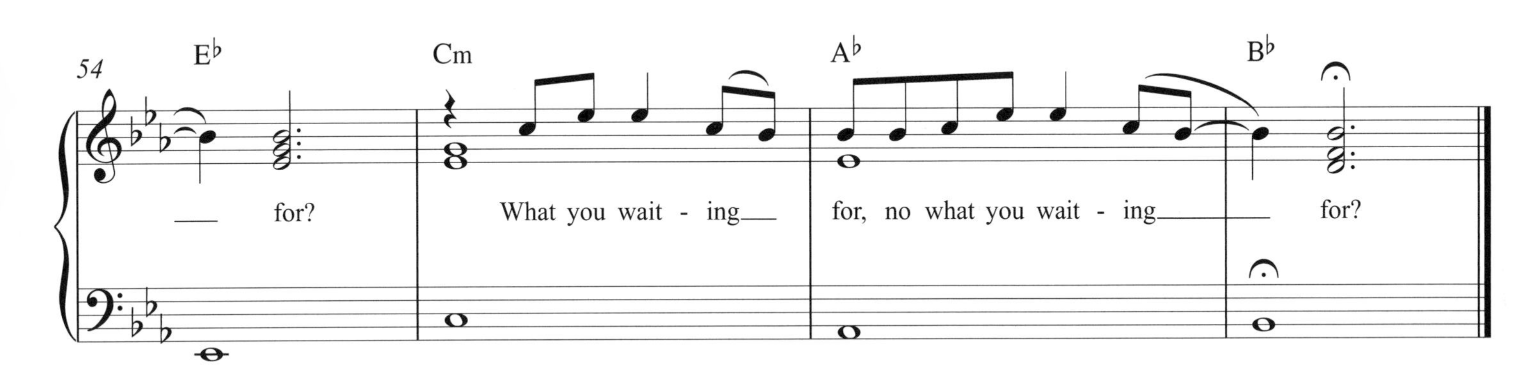
54
E♭
Cm
A♭
B♭
for? What you wait - ing for, no what you wait - ing for?

Blank Space

Words & Music by Max Martin, Taylor Swift & Shellback

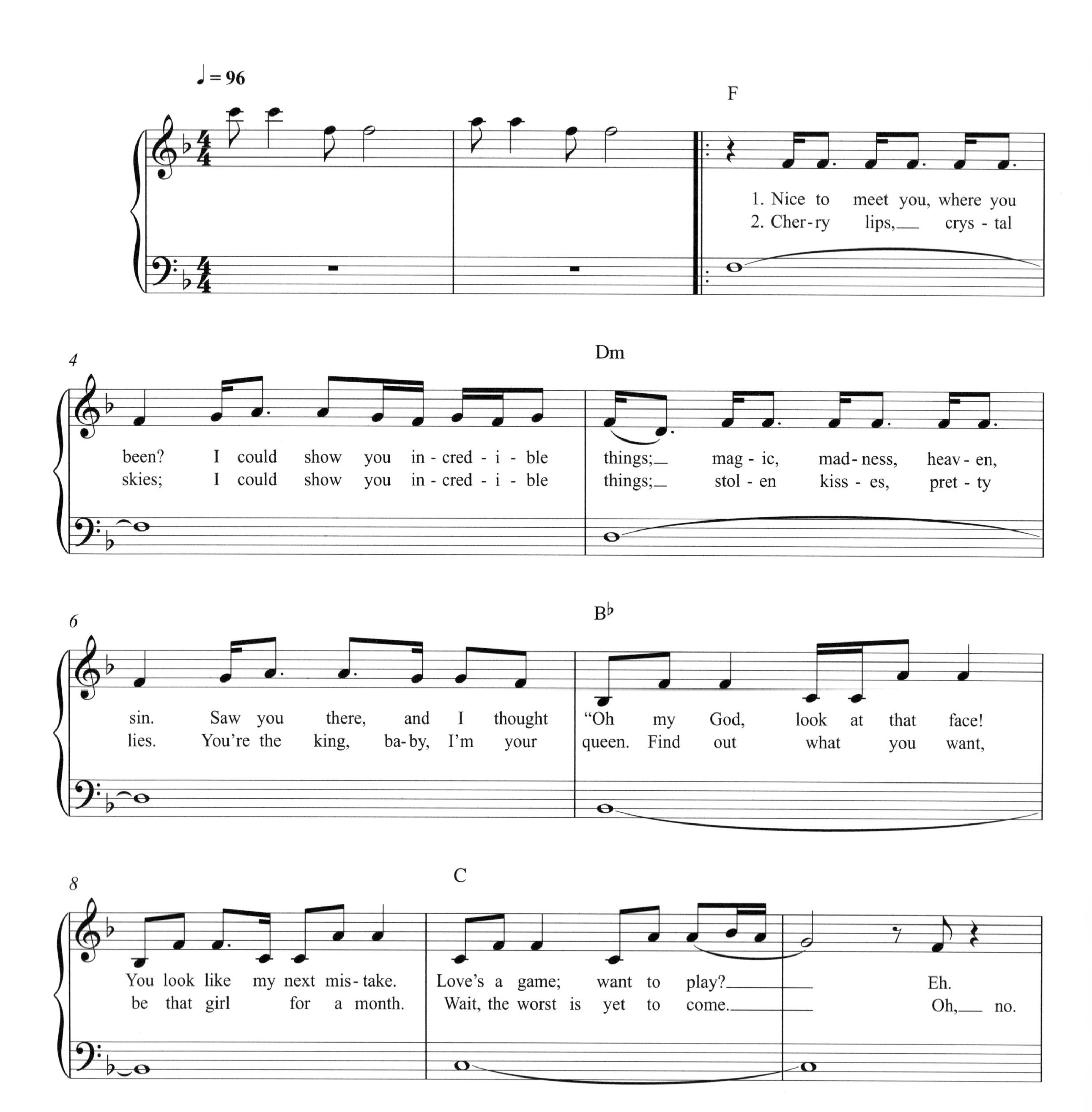

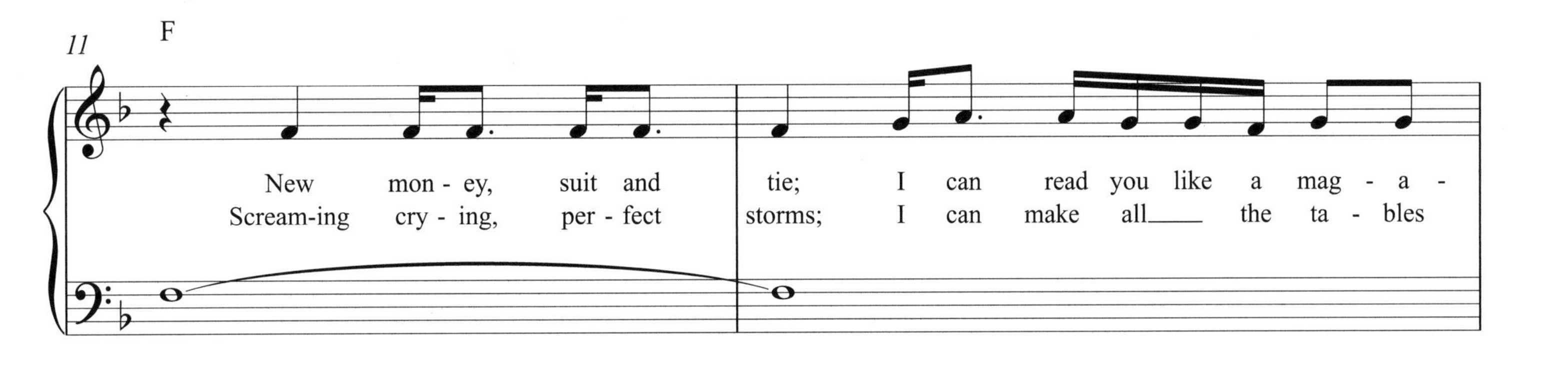
11
F
New mon - ey, suit and tie; I can read you like a mag - a -
Scream-ing cry - ing, per - fect storms; I can make all the ta - bles

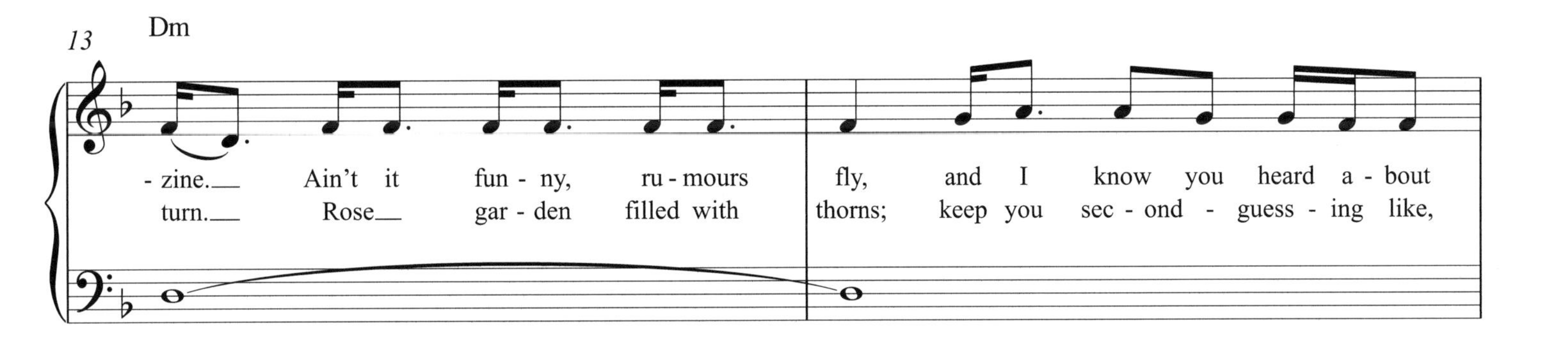
13
Dm
- zine. Ain't it fun - ny, ru - mours fly, and I know you heard a - bout
turn. Rose gar - den filled with thorns; keep you sec - ond - guess - ing like,

15
B♭
me. So hey, let's be friends. I'm dy - ing to see how this one ends.
"Oh my God, who is she?" I get drunk on jeal - ous - y. But

17
C
N.C.
Grab your pass - port and my hand. I can make the bad guys good for a week - end.
you'll come back each time you leave, 'cause darl - ing, I'm a night - mare dressed like a day - dream.

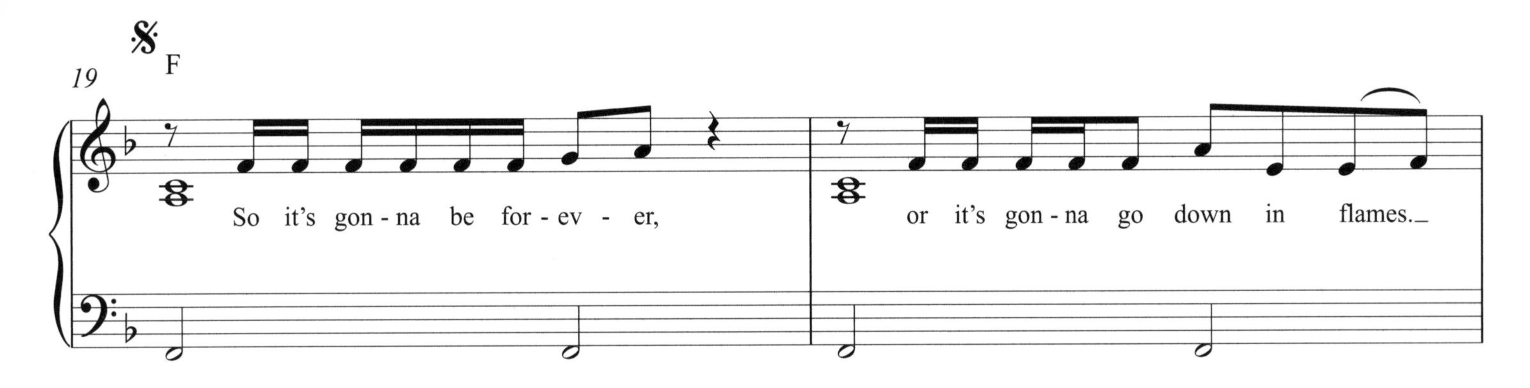
𝄋
19
F
So it's gon - na be for - ev - er, or it's gon - na go down in flames.

21
Dm
You can tell me when it's o - ver, mm,
if the high was worth the pain.
23
Gm7
Got a long list of ex - lov - ers;
they'll tell you I'm in - sane.
25
B♭
'Cause you know I love the play - ers,
and you love the game.
27
F
'Cause we're young and we're reck - less,
we'll take this way too far.
Dm
It-'ll leave you breath - less, mm,
30
or with a nas - ty scar.
Gm7
Got a long list of ex - lov - ers;
they'll tell you I'm in - sane.

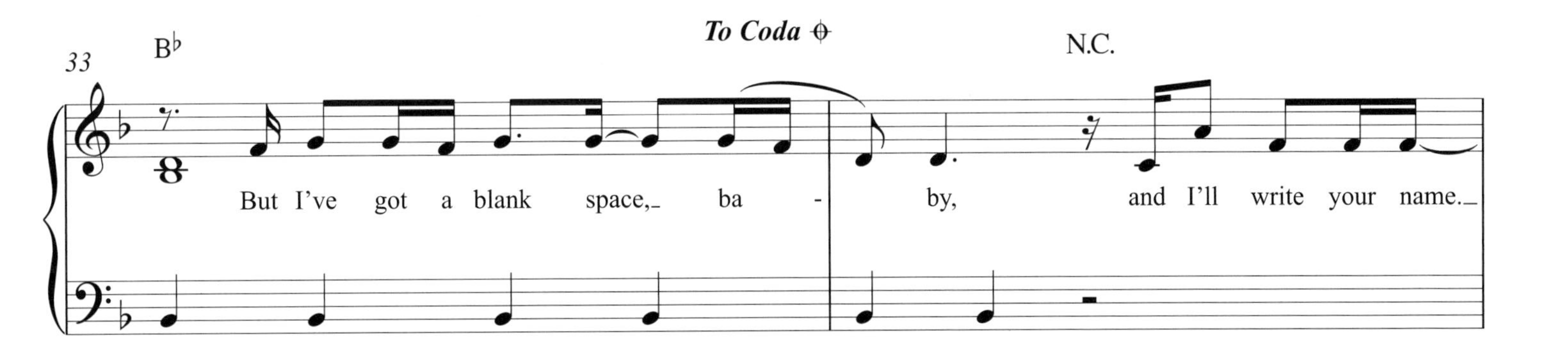
33
B♭
To Coda
N.C.
But I've got a blank space, ba - by, and I'll write your name.

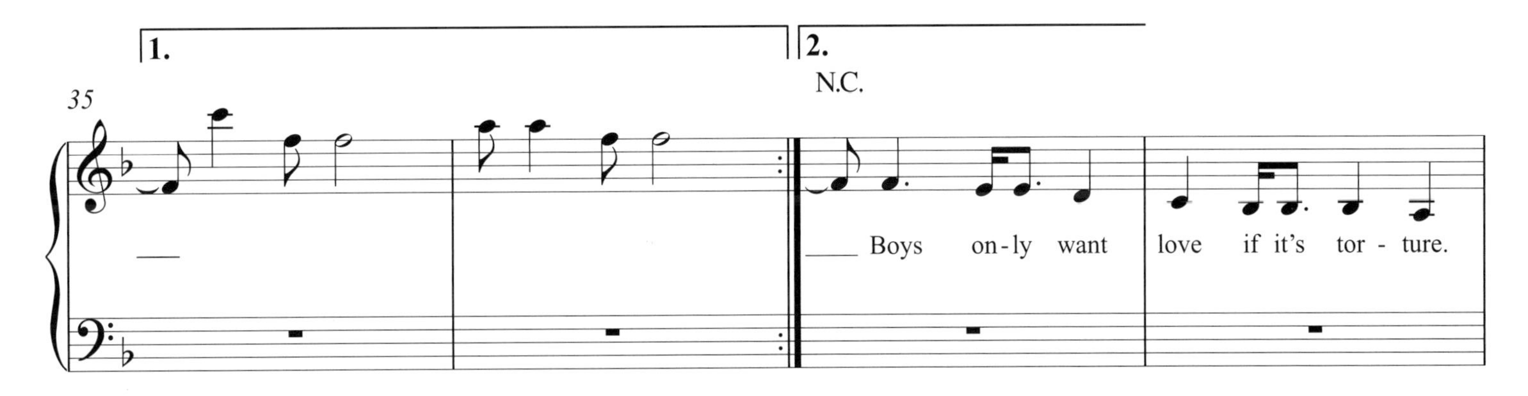
35
1.
2.
N.C.
Boys on-ly want love if it's tor - ture.

39
Don't say I did-n't, say I did-n't warn ya. Boys on-ly want

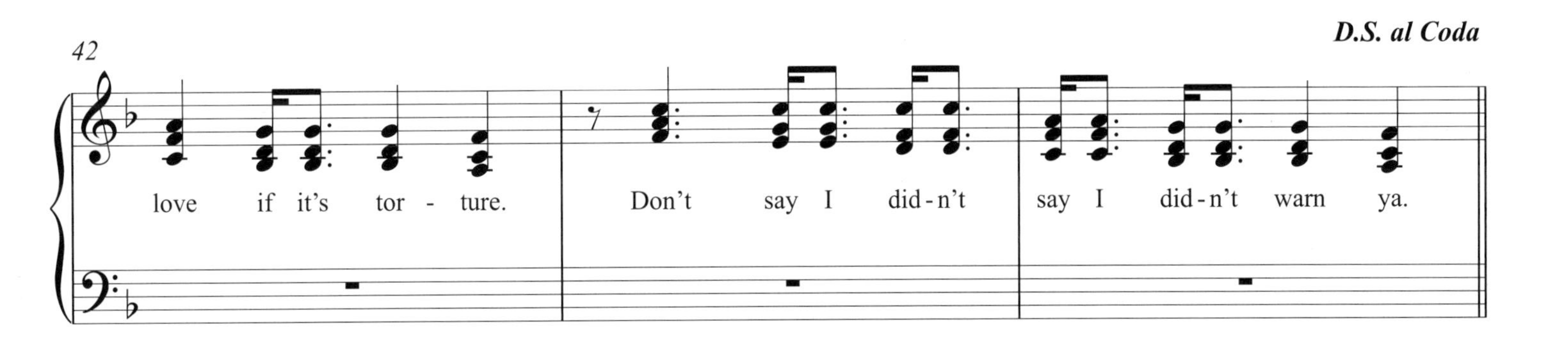
42
D.S. al Coda
love if it's tor - ture. Don't say I did-n't say I did-n't warn ya.

Coda
45
B♭
N.C.
N.C.
Repeat to fade
- by, and I'll write your name.

Drag Me Down

Words & Music by John Ryan, Jamie Scott
& Julian Bunetta

12
Fm
Cm
A♭
be his best. If
I did - n't have you I'd nev - er
see the sun, you
15
B♭
Fm
1° only
Cm
taught me how to be
some - one, yeah.
All my life
18
A♭
B♭
Fm
Cm
you stood by me,
when no one else was
ev - er be - hind me.
All these lights,
22
A♭
B♭
Fm
they can't blind me,
with your love no -
bod - y can drag me
25
Cm
A♭
B♭
Fm
All my life
(down.)
you stood by me
when no one else was
ev - er be - hind me.

29
Cm
A♭
B♭
N.C.
All these_ lights, they can't blind me, with your_ love no - bod - y can drag me

33
Cm
A♭maj7
B♭
Fm
down. No-bod-y, no-bod - y, no - bod - y can drag_ me

37
Cm
A♭maj7
B♭
Fm
down. No-bod-y, no-bod - y, no- bod-y can drag_ me

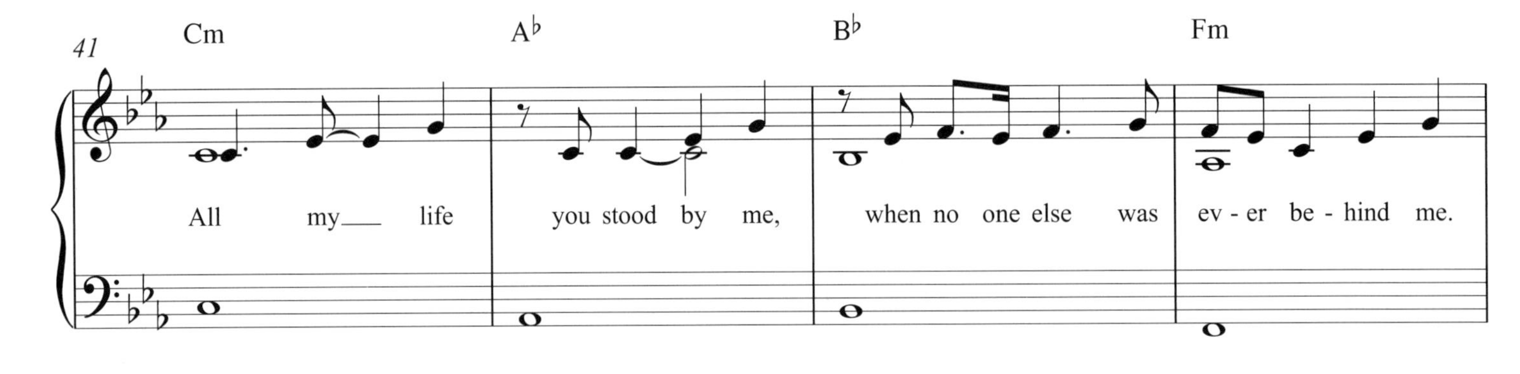
41
Cm
A♭
B♭
Fm
All my___ life you stood by me, when no one else was ev - er be - hind me.

45
Cm
A♭
B♭
Fm
All these_ lights, they can't blind me, with your_ love no - bod - y can drag me

49
Cm
A♭
B♭
Fm
All my__ life you stood by me when no one else was ev - er be - hind me.
down.
53
Cm
A♭
B♭
N.C.
All these__ lights they can't blind me with your__ love no - bod - y can drag me
57
Cm
A♭maj7
B♭
down. No - bod - y, no - bod - y, no -
60
Fm
Cm
A♭maj7
-bod - y can drag__ me down. No - bod - y, no - bod -
63
B♭
Fm
N.C.
- y, no - bod - y can drag__ me down.

Flashlight

Words & Music by Jason Moore, Sia Furler,
Sam Smith, Christian Guzman & Mario Mejia

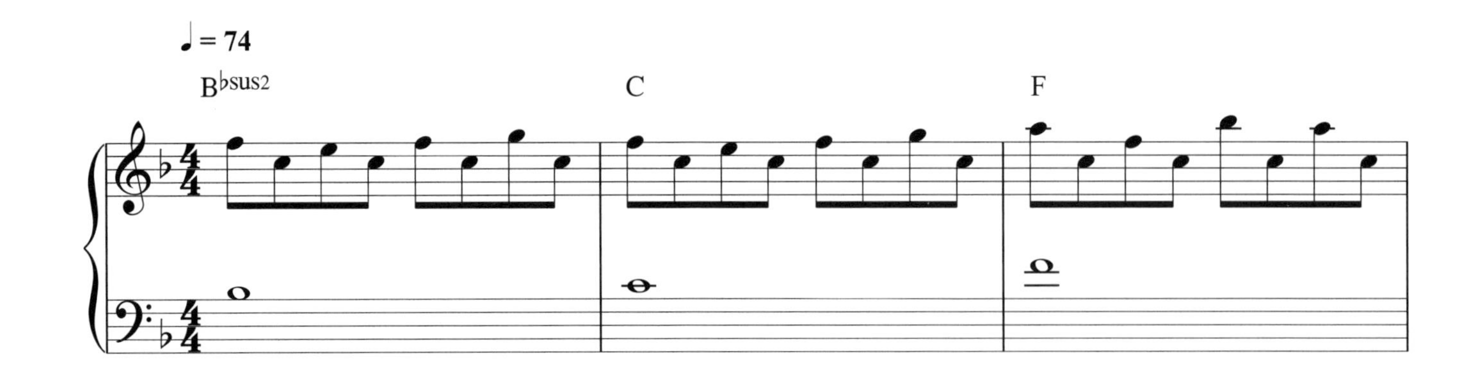

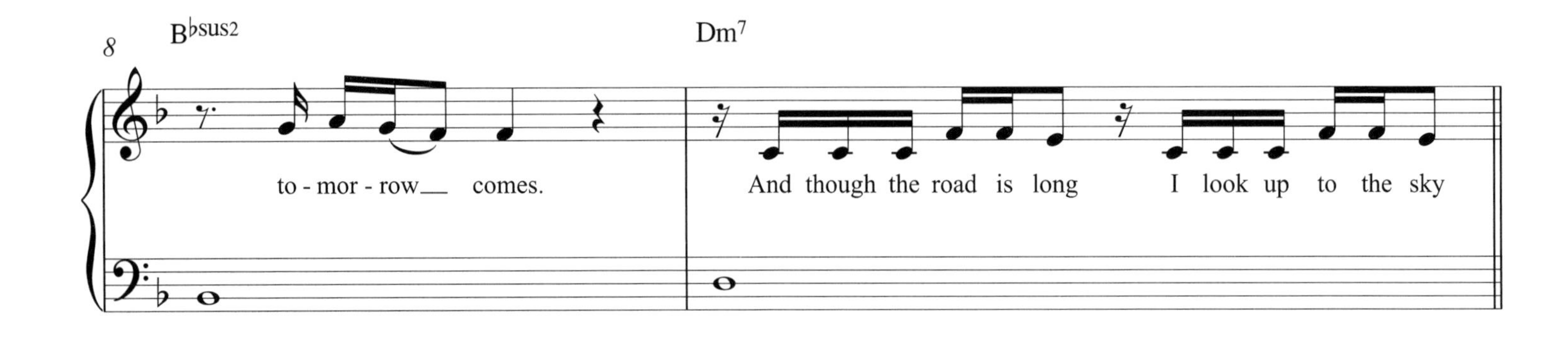

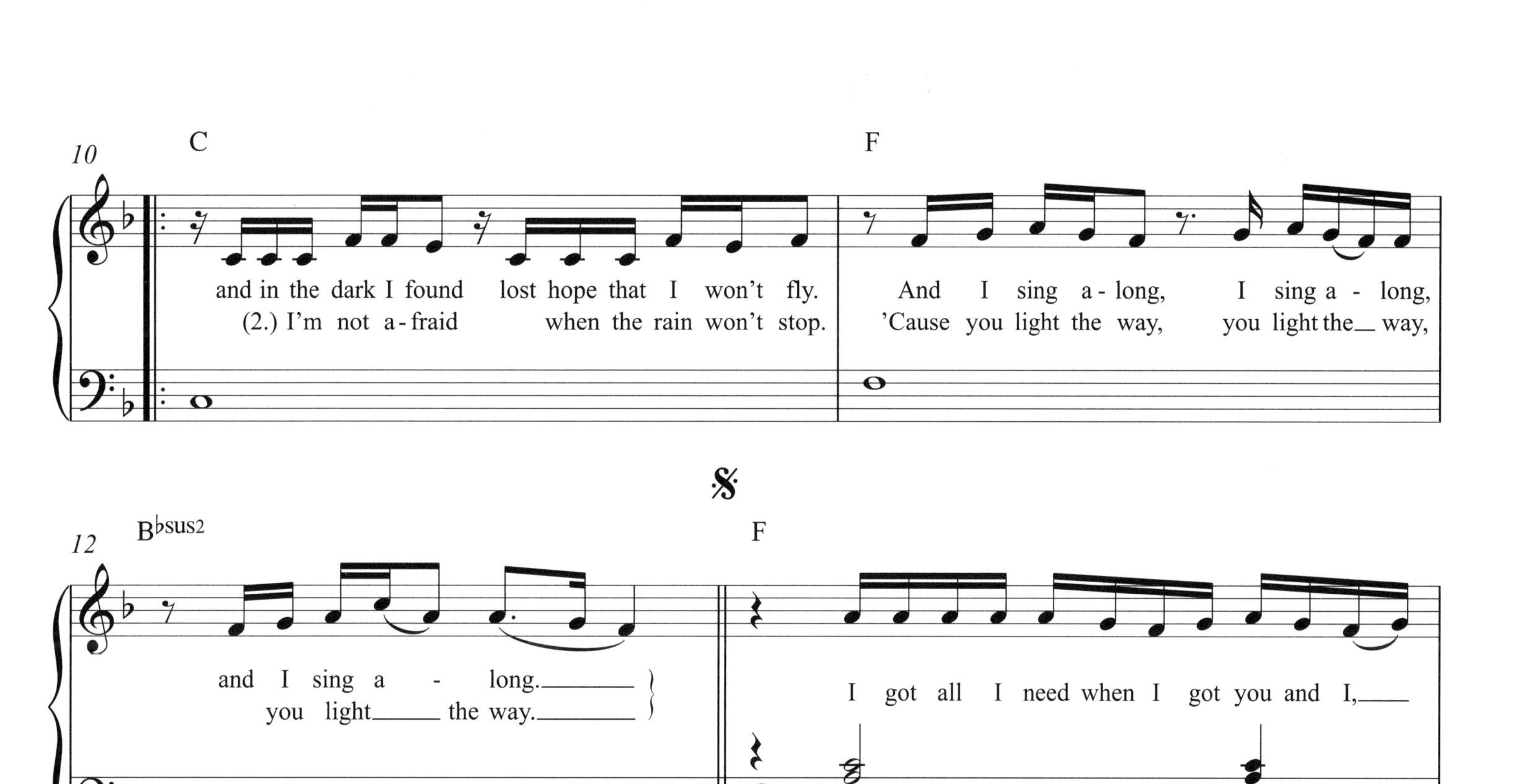
10
C
F
and in the dark I found lost hope that I won't fly.
(2.) I'm not a-fraid when the rain won't stop.
And I sing a - long, I sing a - long,
'Cause you light the way, you light the way,
𝄋
12
B♭sus2
and I sing a - long.
you light the way.
F
I got all I need when I got you and I,

14
C
Dm
I look a-round me and see a sweet life.
I'm stuck in the dark but you're my flash - light.
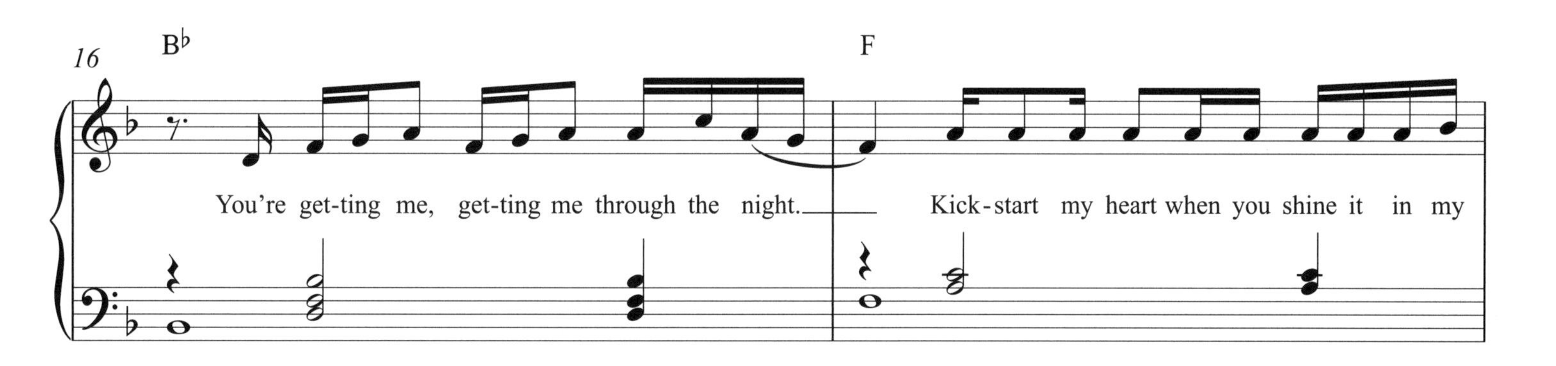
16
B♭
F
You're get-ting me, get-ting me through the night.
Kick-start my heart when you shine it in my

18
C
Dm
eyes, I can't lie, it's a sweet
life. I'm stuck in the dark but you're my flash - light.

1, 3.
20
B♭
F
You're get-ting me, get-ting me through the night.
'Cause you're my flash -

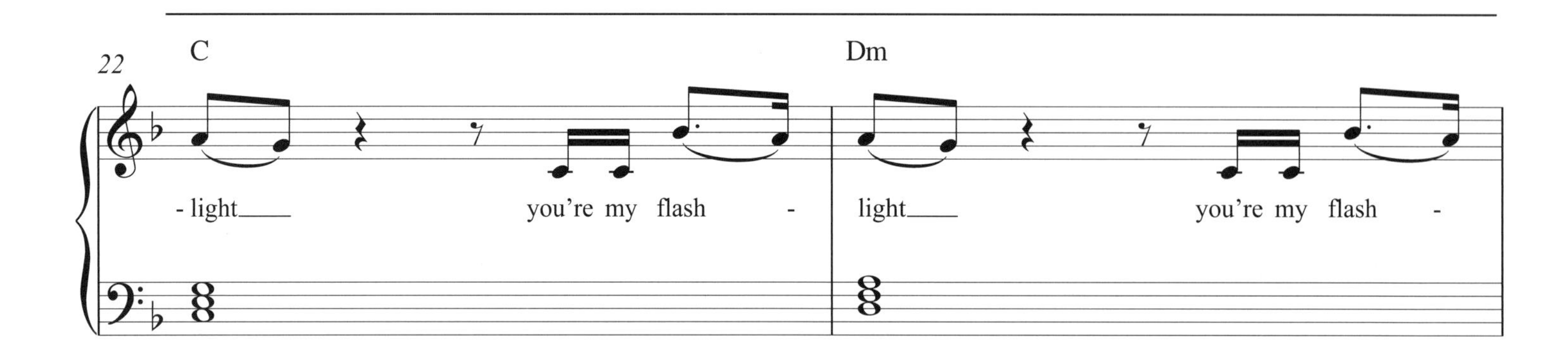
22
C
Dm
- light you're my flash - light you're my flash -

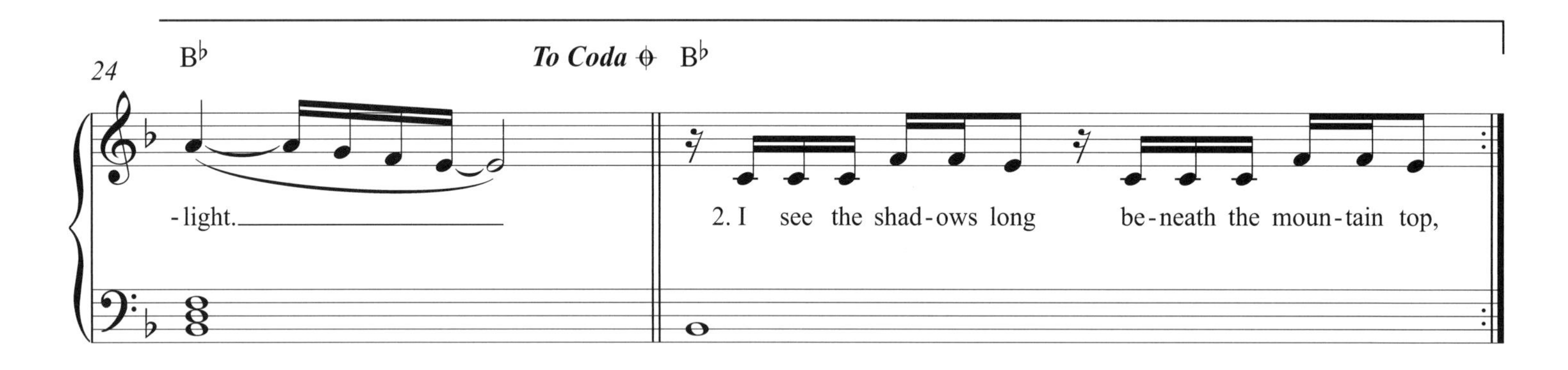
24
B♭
To Coda
B♭
- light.
2. I see the shad-ows long be-neath the moun-tain top,

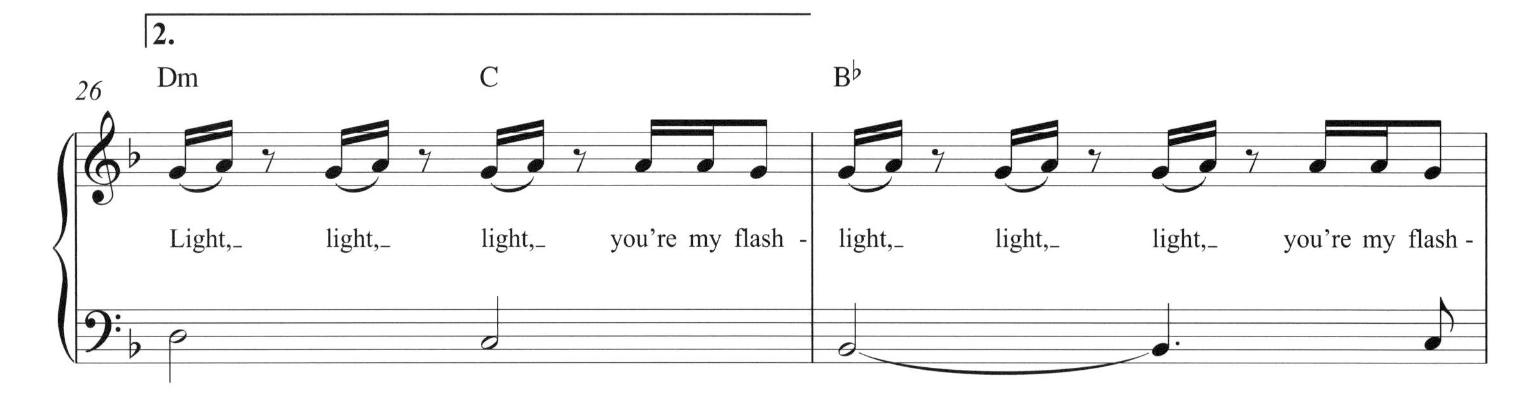
2.
26
Dm
C
B♭
Light, light, light, you're my flash - light, light, light, you're my flash -

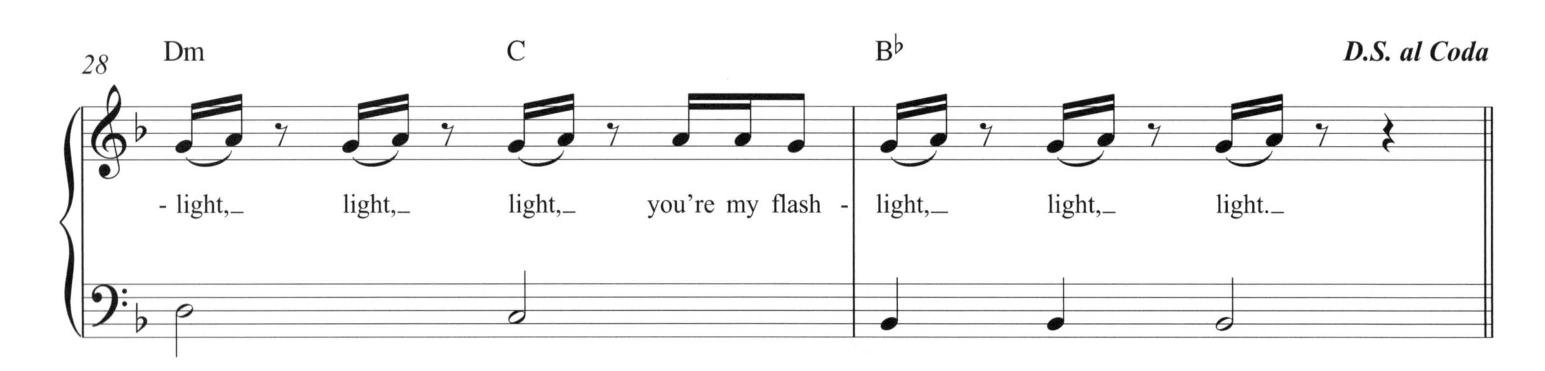
28
Dm
C
B♭
D.S. al Coda
- light, light, light, you're my flash - light, light, light.

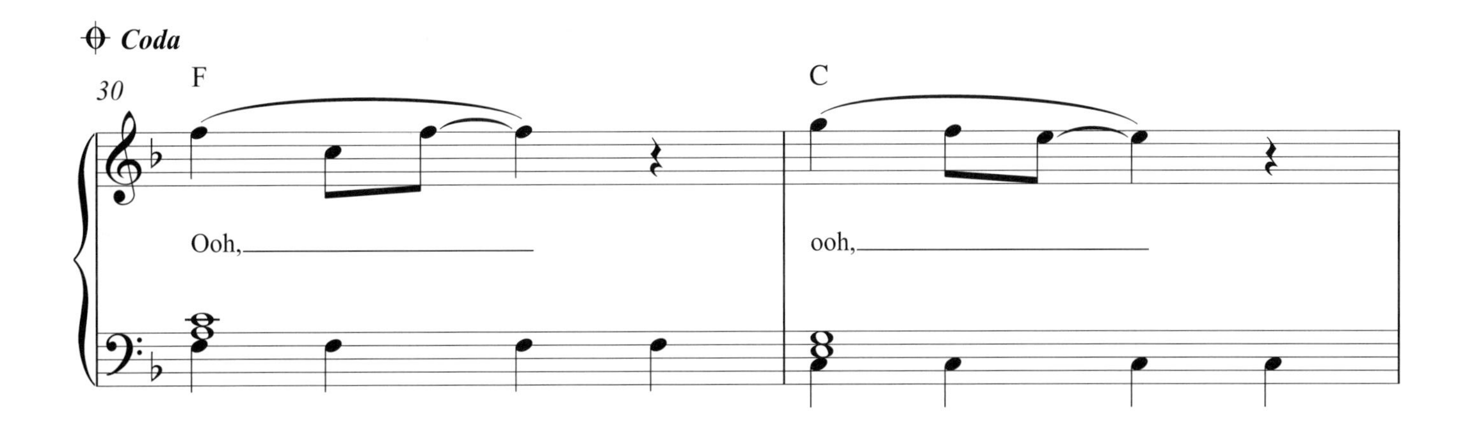
Coda
30
F
C
Ooh,
ooh,

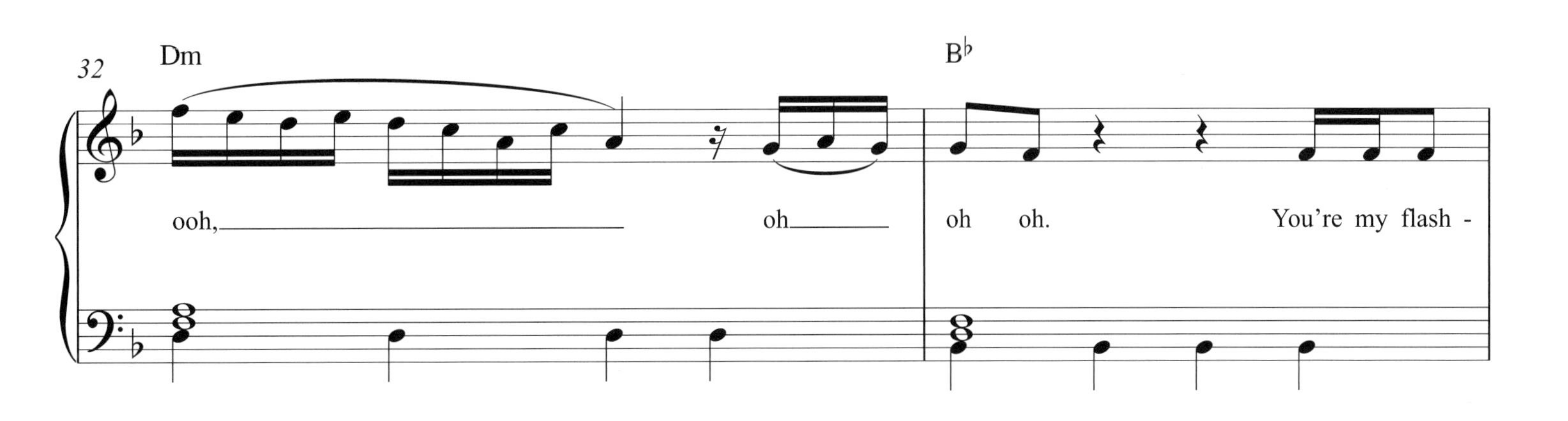
32
Dm
B♭
ooh,
oh
oh oh.
You're my flash -

34
F
C
- light,
light,
light,
you're my flash -
light,
light,
light,
yeah,

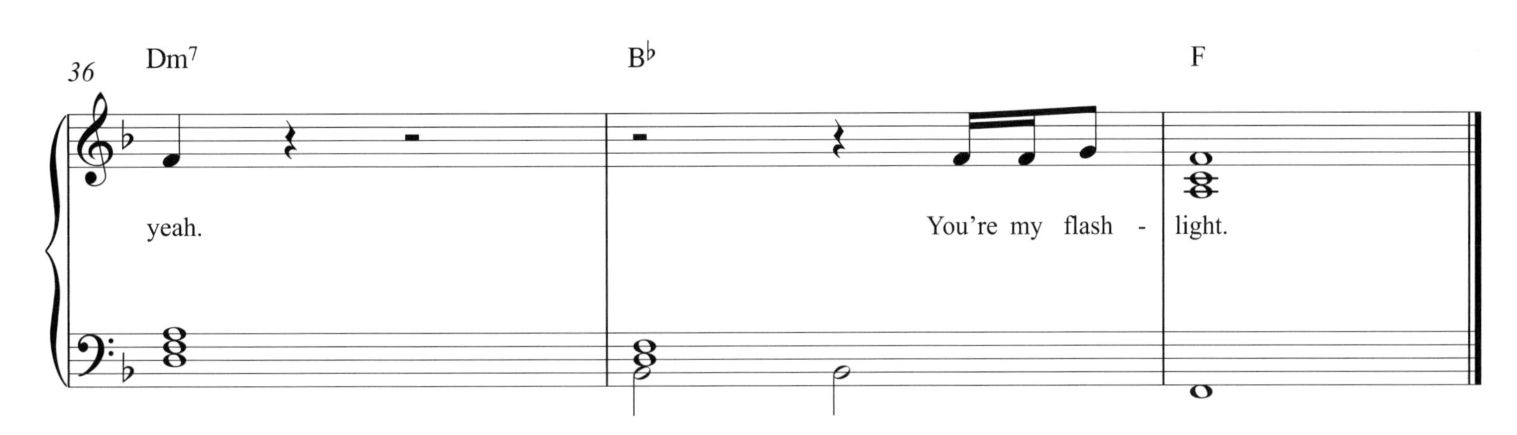
36
Dm7
B♭
F
yeah.
You're my flash -
light.

FourFiveSeconds

Words & Music by Rihanna, Paul McCartney
& Kanye West

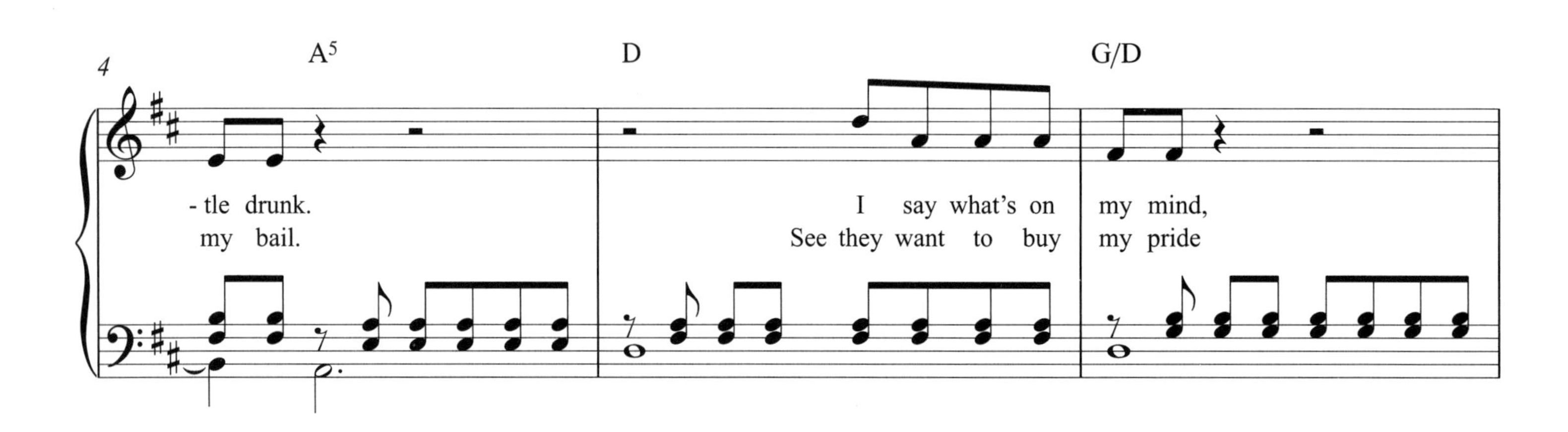

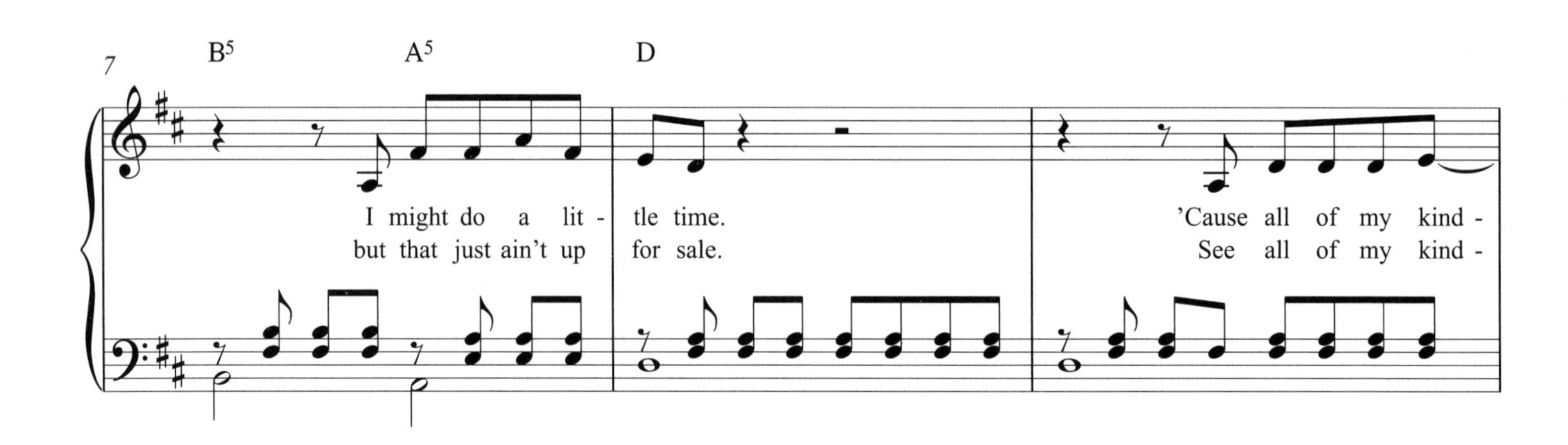

10
G/D
B5
A5
To Coda ⊕
- ness
- ness
is ta - ken for weak - ness. Now I'm
13
D
G/D
D
four, five se - conds from wild - in' and we got three more days till Fri -
16
G/D
- day. I'm just try'n - a make it back home by Mon - day morn - in' I swear.
19
B5
A5
D
I wish some - bod - y would tell me, ooh, that's all I want. 2. Woke up an
22
G/D
D
G/D
op - ti - mist. Sun was shin - ing, I'm pos - i - tive.

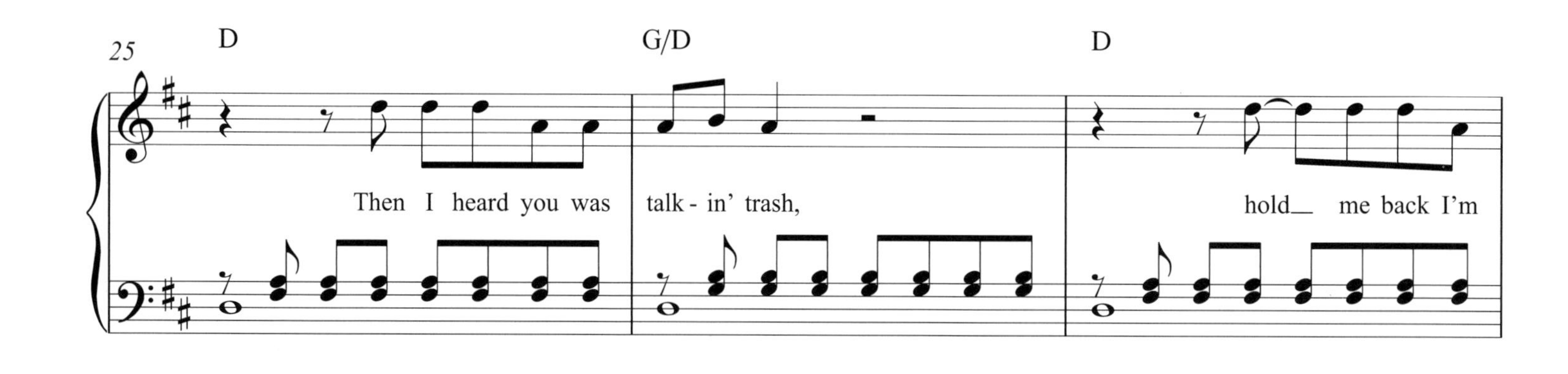
25
D
G/D
D
Then I heard you was talk - in' trash, hold__ me back I'm

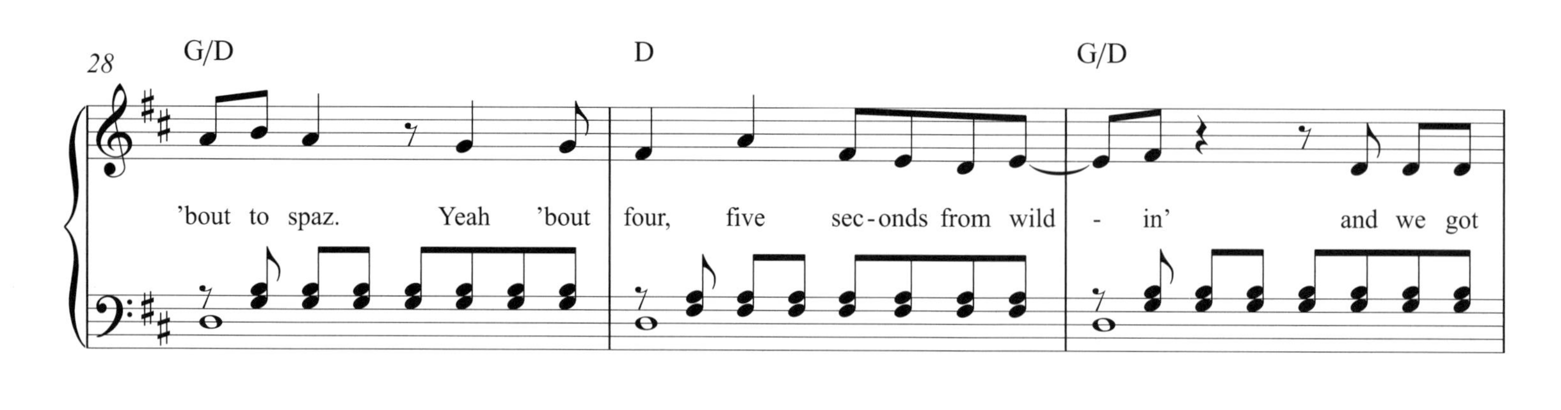
28
G/D
D
G/D
'bout to spaz. Yeah 'bout four, five sec - onds from wild - in' and we got

31
D
G/D
three more days__ till Fri - day. I'm try'n - a make it back home__ by Mon-

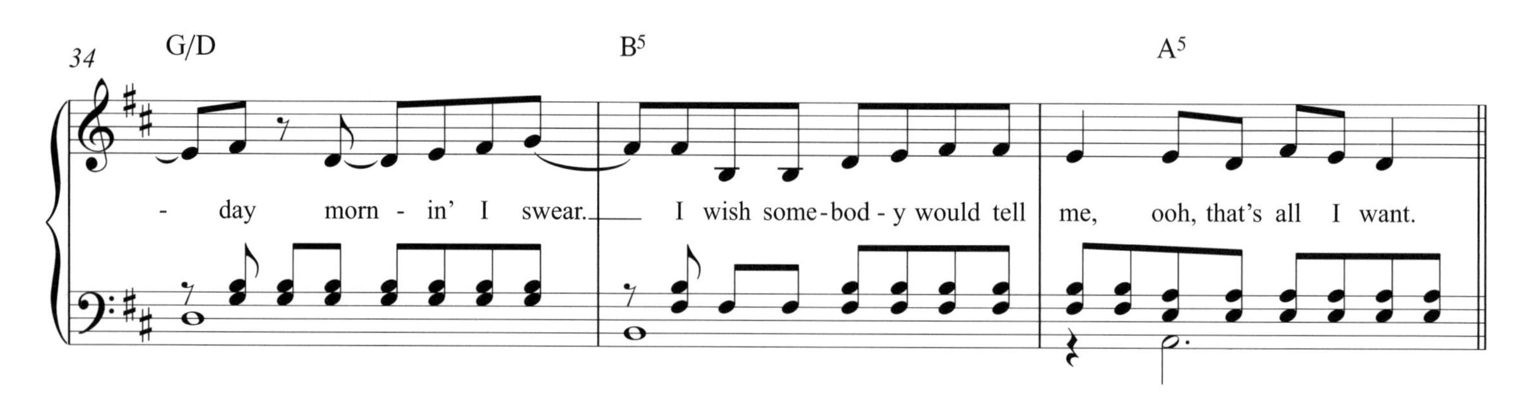
34
G/D
B5
A5
- day morn - in' I swear.__ I wish some-bod - y would tell me, ooh, that's all I want.

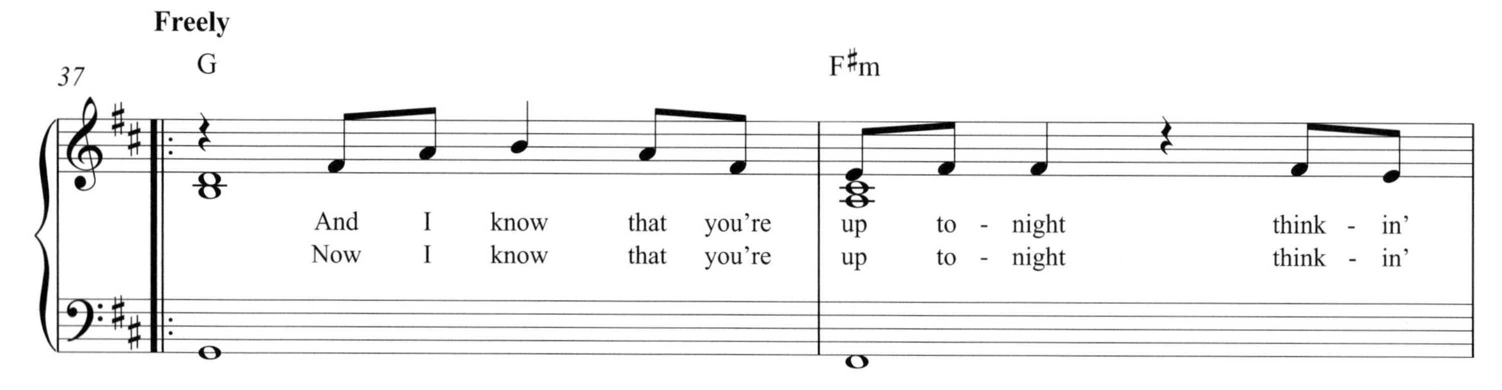
Freely
37
G
F♯m
And I know that you're up to - night think - in'
Now I know that you're up to - night think - in'

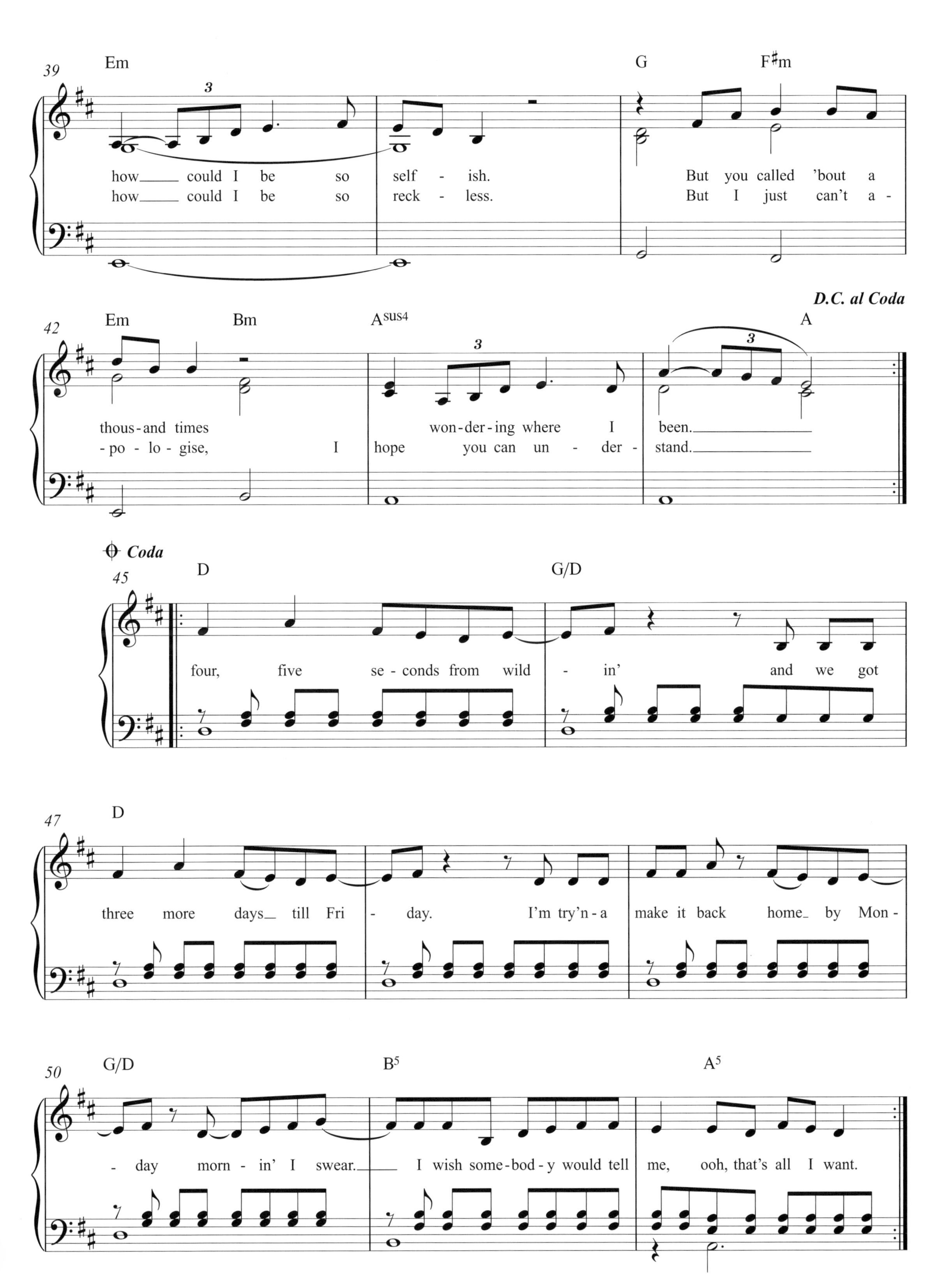
39
Em
G
F♯m
how could I be so selfish.
how could I be so reckless.
But you called 'bout a
But I just can't a-
D.C. al Coda
42
Em
Bm
Asus4
A
thous-and times won-der-ing where I been.
-po-lo-gise, I hope you can un-der-stand.
Coda
45
D
G/D
four, five se-conds from wild-in' and we got
47
D
three more days till Fri-day. I'm try'n-a make it back home by Mon-
50
G/D
B5
A5
-day morn-in' I swear. I wish some-bod-y would tell me, ooh, that's all I want.

Cheerleader

Words & Music by Clifton Dillon, Sly Dunbar,
Mark Antonio Bradford, Omar Samuel Pasely & Ryan Dillon

15
E
B
A
oth - er girls are tempt - ing but I'm
emp - ty when you're gone. And they say:
17
E
A
B
A
"Do you need me?
Do you think I'm pret - ty? Do I
19
E
A
B
A
make you feel like cheat - ing?" And I'm:
"No, not real - ly." 'Cause
21
E
A
B
A
E
A
oh, I think that I found my - self a cheer - lead - er.
She is al - ways right there
24
B
A
E
A
B
A
when I need her.
Oh, I think that I found my - self a cheer - lead - er.

1.
27
E A B A
She is al - ways right there when I need her. She

29
E B A E
walks like a mo-del. She grants my wish-es like a ge-nie in a bot-tle.

32
B A E B A
(Yeah, yeah.) I'm the wiz-ard of love and I got the ma-gic wand. All these

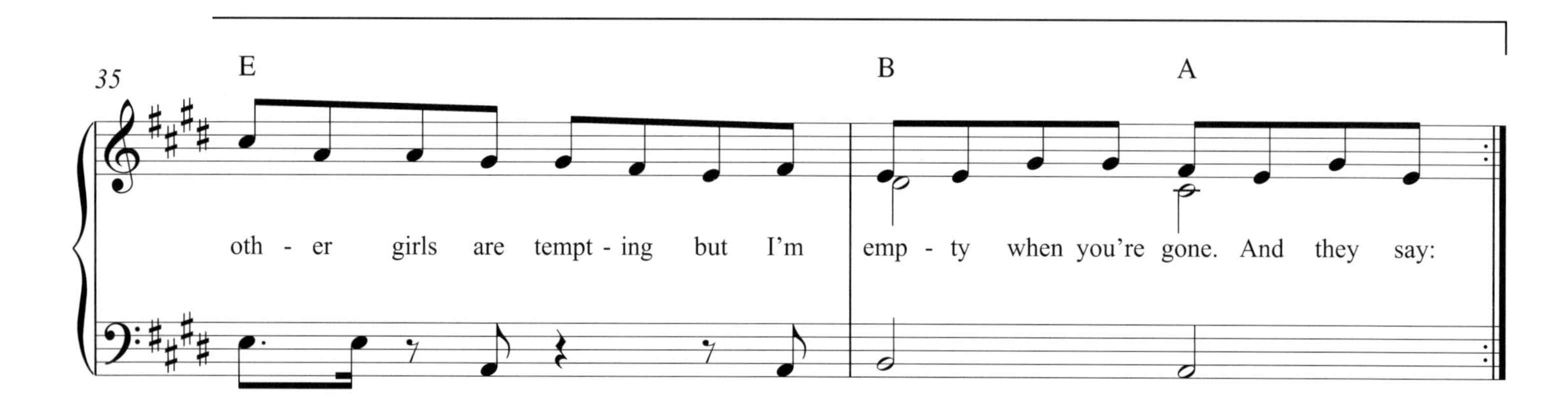
35
E B A
oth - er girls are tempt - ing but I'm emp - ty when you're gone. And they say:

2, 3.
B
A
when I
need
her.
E
B
A
E
To Coda
B
A
E
B
A
E
E
B
A
E
B
A
Ooh.
She gives me

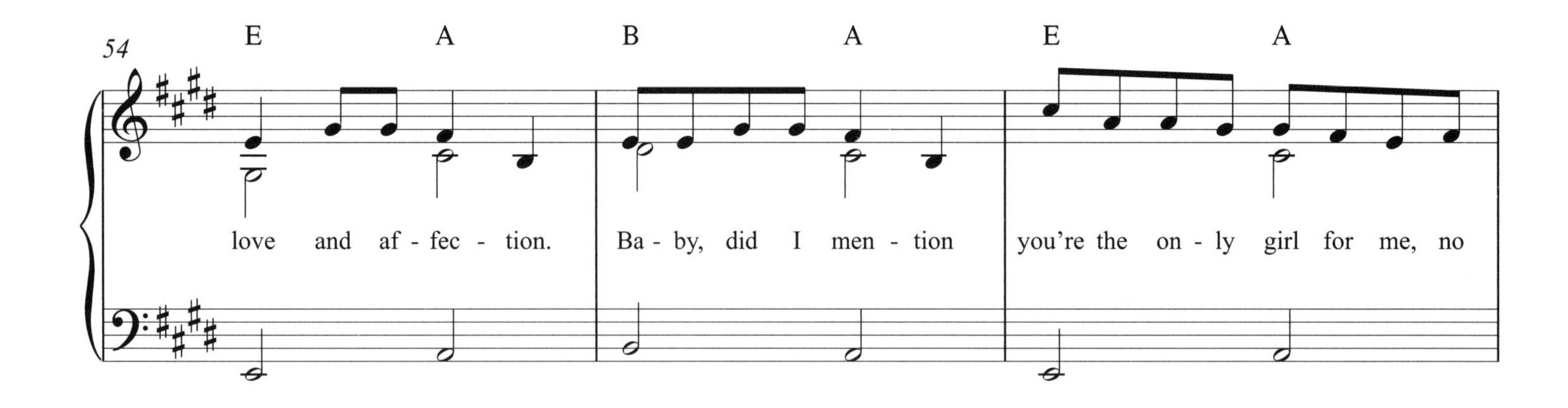
54
E A B A E A
love and af - fec - tion. Ba - by, did I men - tion you're the on - ly girl for me, no

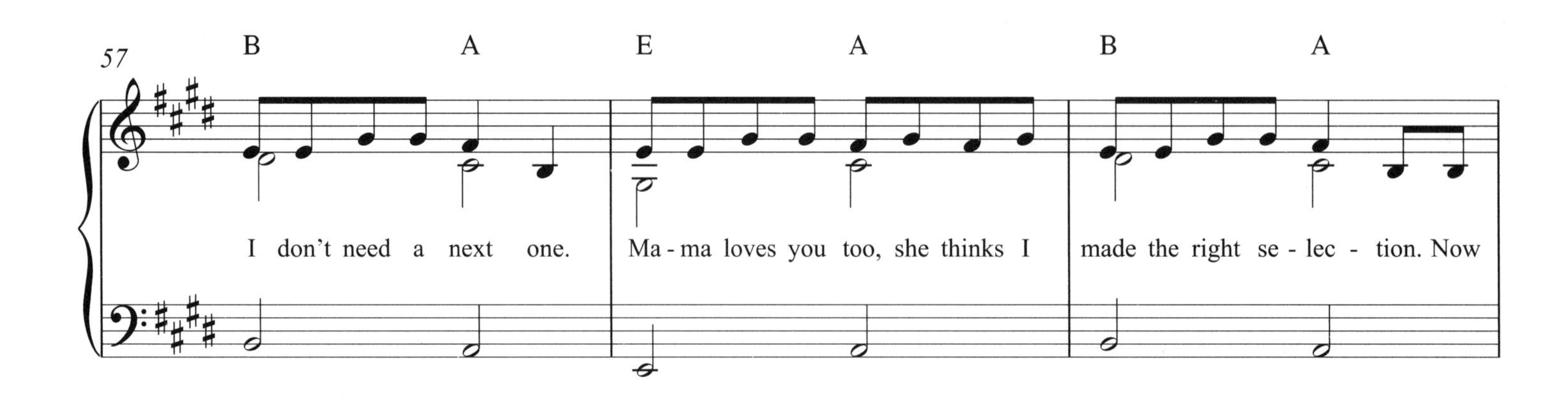
57
B A E A B A
I don't need a next one. Ma - ma loves you too, she thinks I made the right se - lec - tion. Now

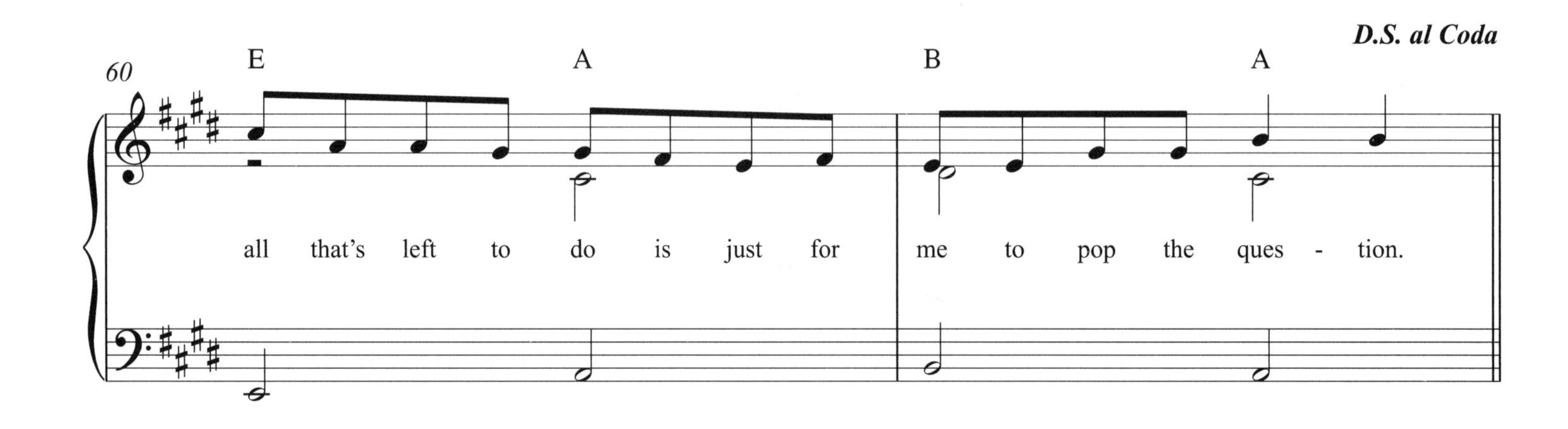
D.S. al Coda
60
E A B A
all that's left to do is just for me to pop the ques - tion.

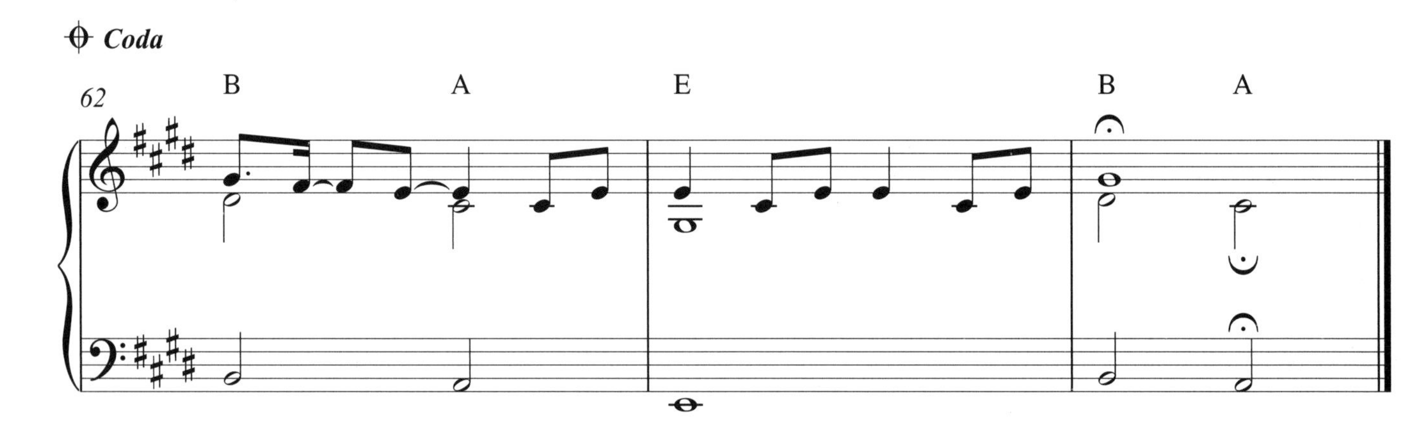
Coda
62
B A E B A

Hold Back The River

Words & Music by Iain Archer & James Bay

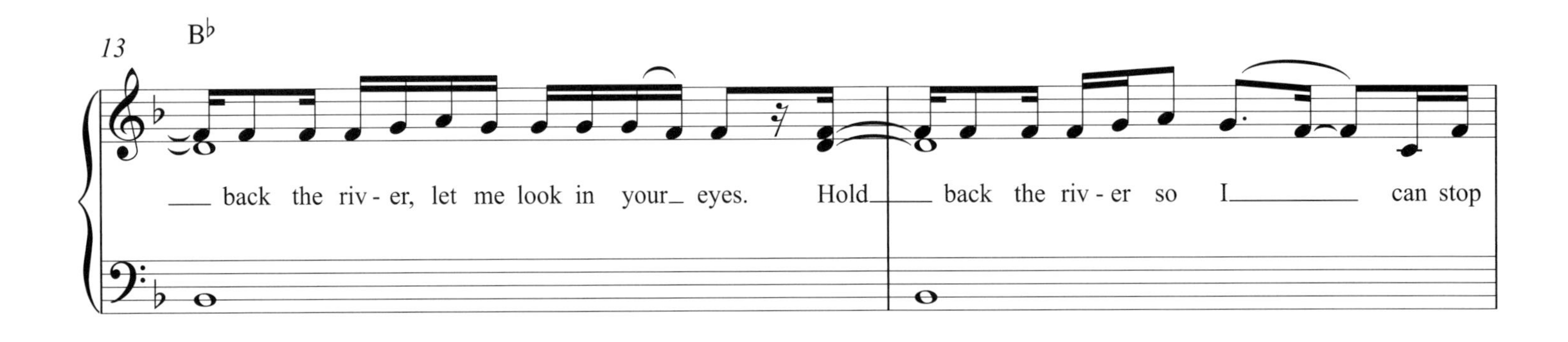
13
B♭
back the riv - er, let me look in your eyes. Hold back the riv - er so I can stop

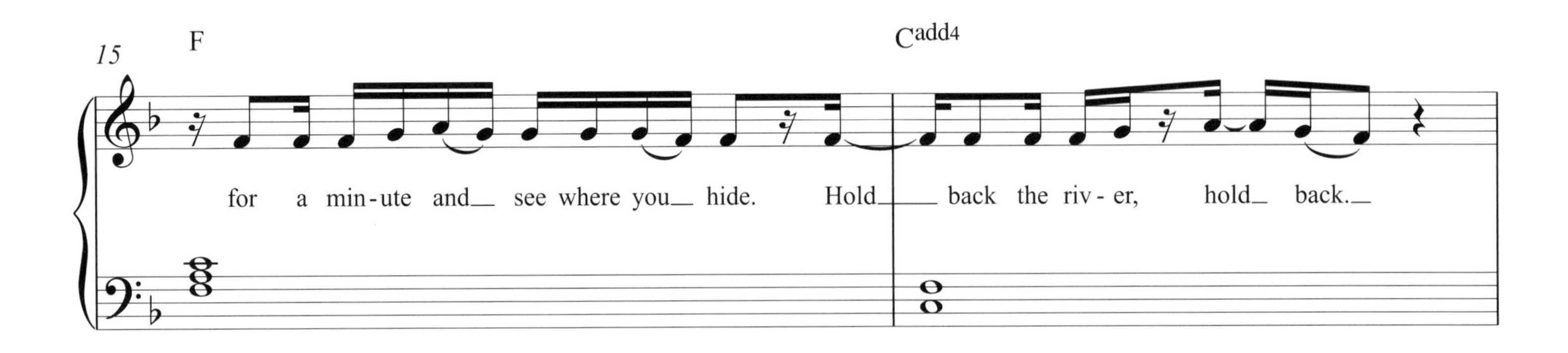
15
F
Cadd4
for a min-ute and see where you hide. Hold back the riv - er, hold back.

17
Dm F Dm F B♭ F B♭
2. Once up - on a diff - 'rent life we rode

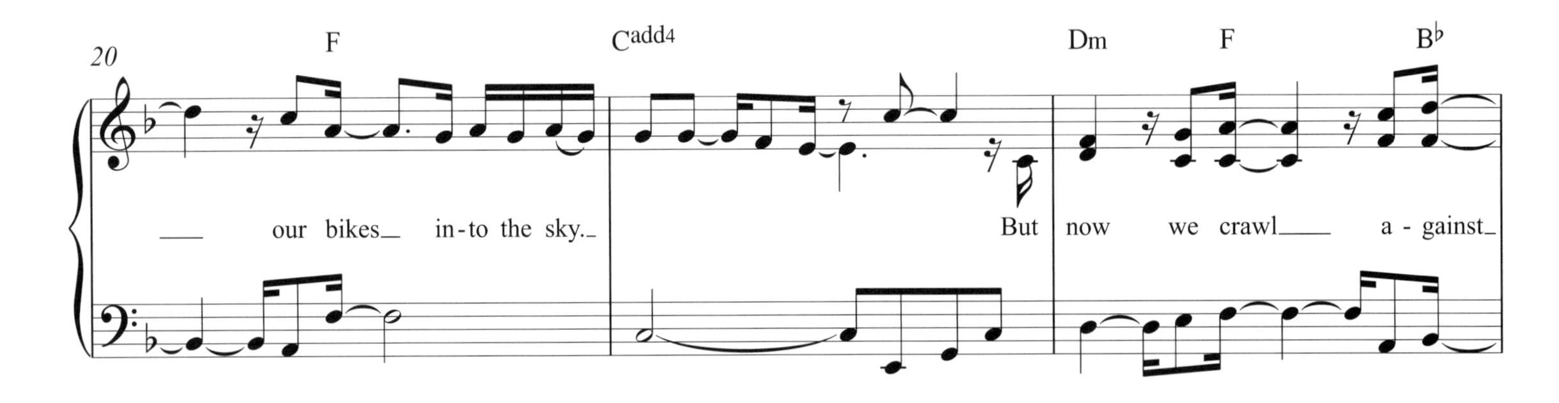
20
F Cadd4 Dm F B♭
our bikes in-to the sky. But now we crawl a - gainst

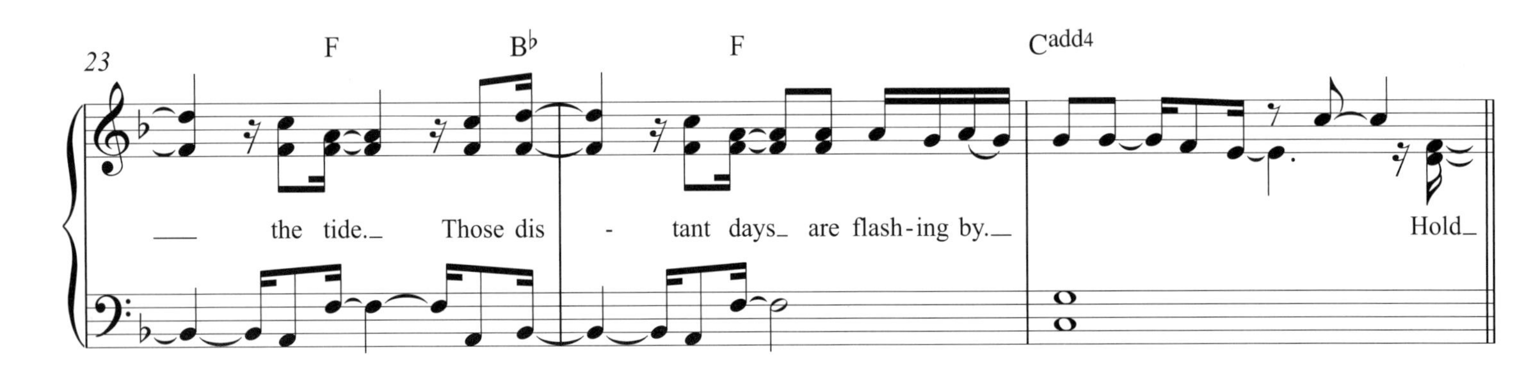
23
F B♭ F Cadd4
the tide. Those dis - tant days are flash-ing by. Hold

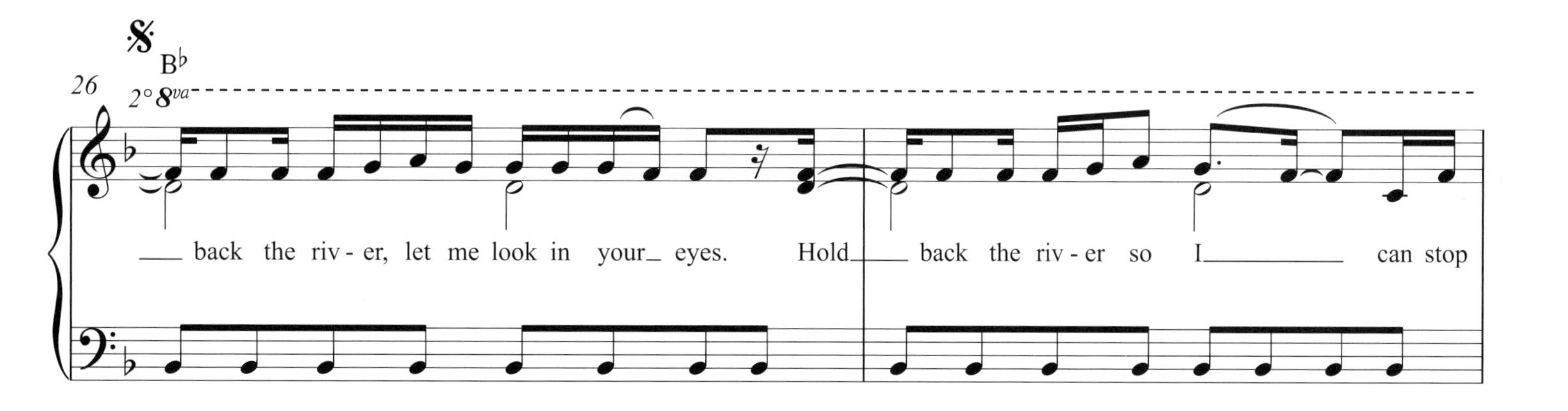
26
B♭
2° 8va
back the riv - er, let me look in your eyes. Hold back the riv - er so I can stop

28
F
(8)
Cadd11
for a min-ute and be by your side. Hold back the riv - er, hold back. Hold

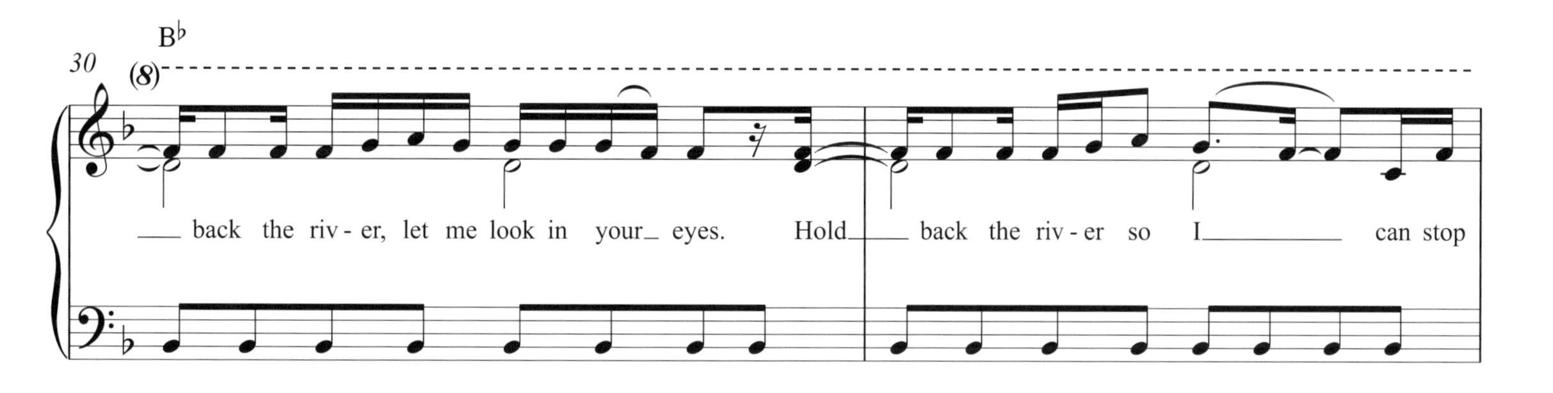
30
B♭
(8)
back the riv - er, let me look in your eyes. Hold back the riv - er so I can stop

32
F
(8)
Cadd11
To Coda
for a min-ute and see where you hide. Hold back the riv - er, hold back.

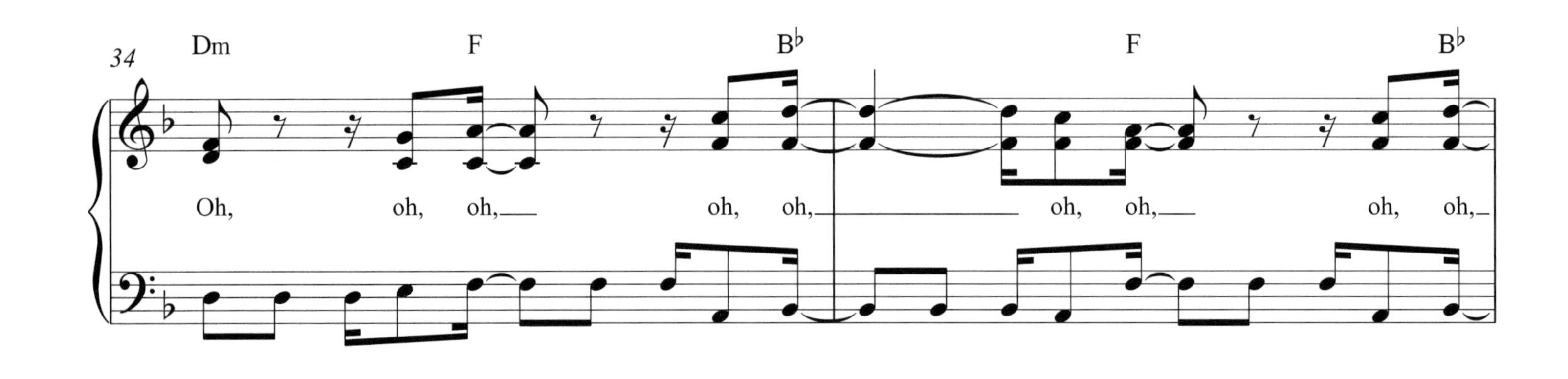
34
Dm
F
B♭
F
B♭
Oh, oh, oh, oh, oh, oh, oh, oh, oh,

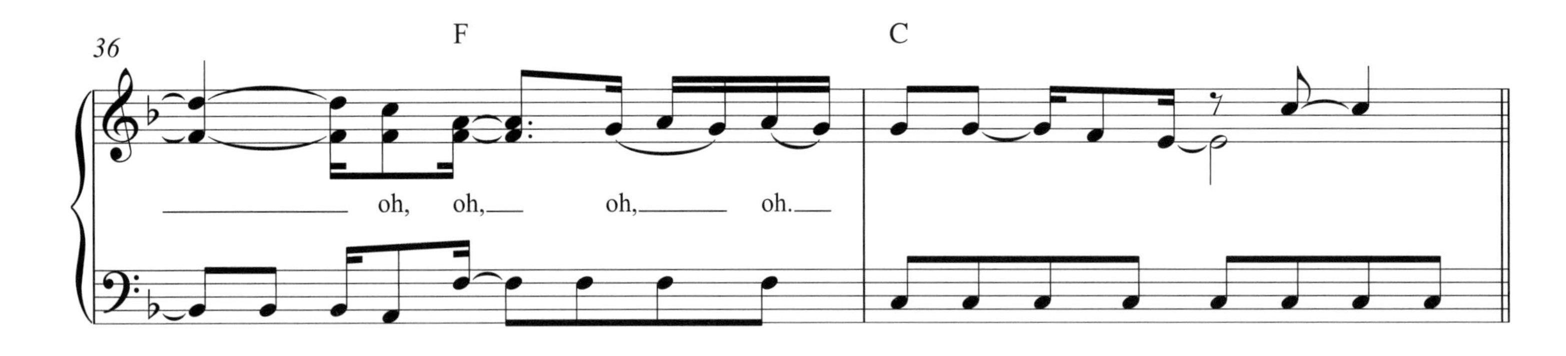
36
F
C
oh, oh, oh, oh.

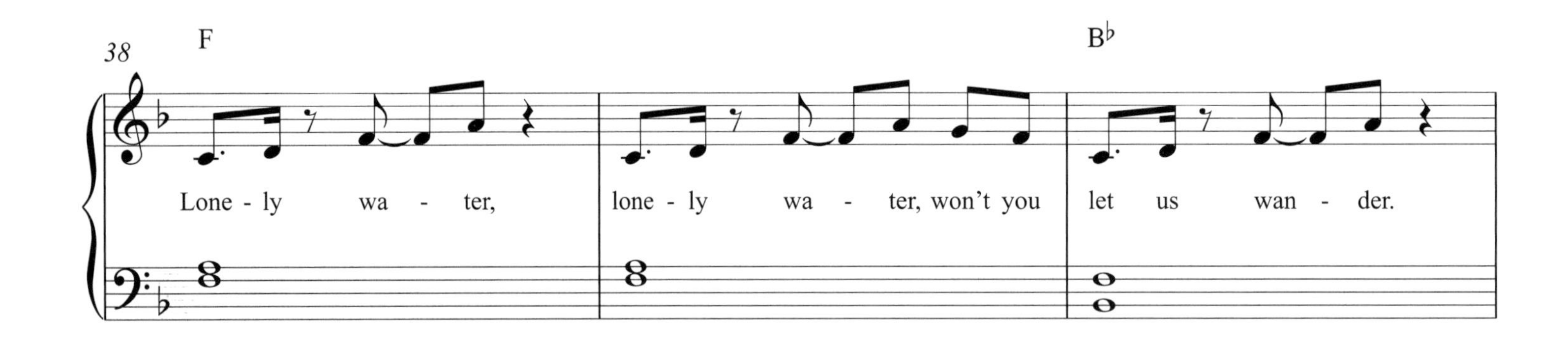
38
F
B♭
Lone - ly wa - ter, lone - ly wa - ter, won't you let us wan - der.

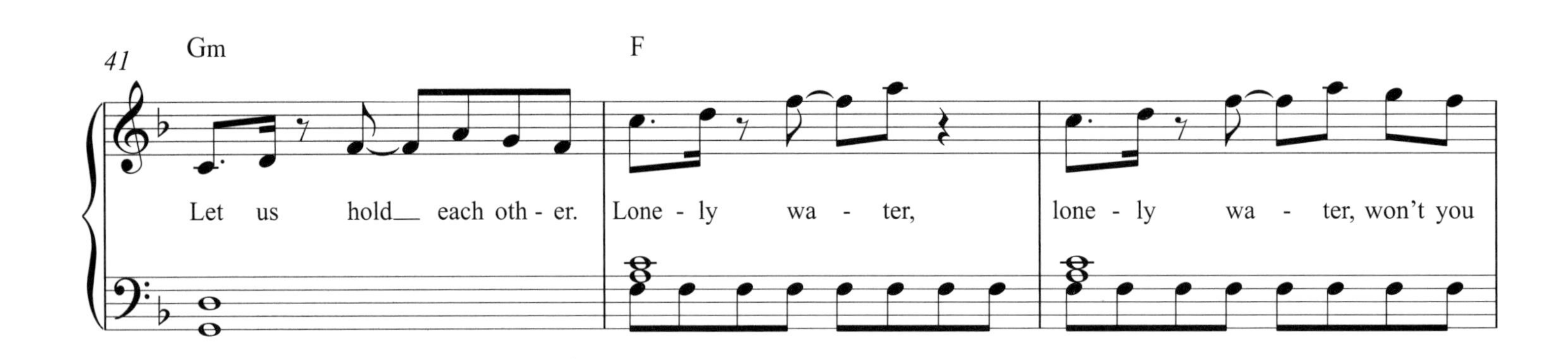
41
Gm
F
Let us hold each oth - er. Lone - ly wa - ter, lone - ly wa - ter, won't you

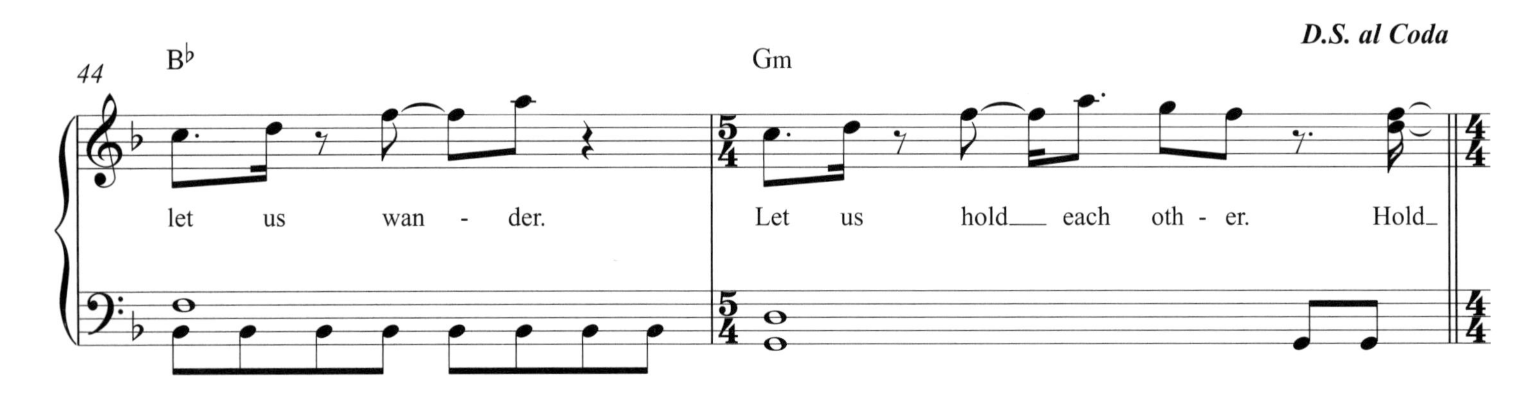
D.S. al Coda
44
B♭
Gm
let us wan - der. Let us hold each oth - er. Hold

Coda
46
F
Lone - ly wa - ter,
lone - ly wa - ter, won't you
48
B♭
let us wan - der.
Gm
C
Let us hold each oth - er.
F
Lone - ly wa - ter,
51
lone - ly wa - ter, won't you
B♭
let us wan - der.
53
Gm
Let us hold each oth - er.
Dm
F
56
B♭/F
F
B♭/F
F
Csus4

Hold My Hand

Words & Music by Ina Wroldsen, Jack Patterson,
Jess Glynne & Janee Bennett

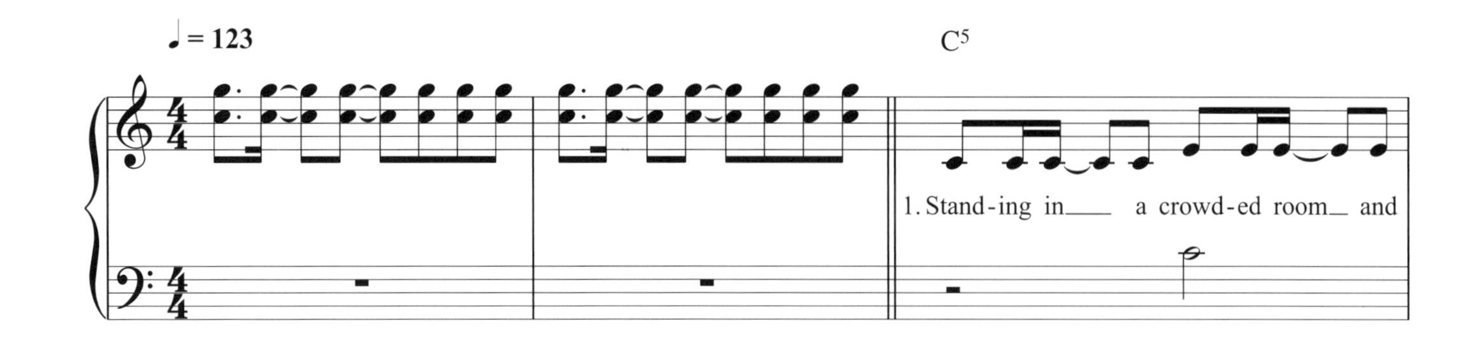
♩ = 123
C5
1. Stand-ing in a crowd-ed room and

4
I can't see your face. (Ooh
ooh ooh ooh, ooh ooh
ooh ooh ooh, ooh ooh.)

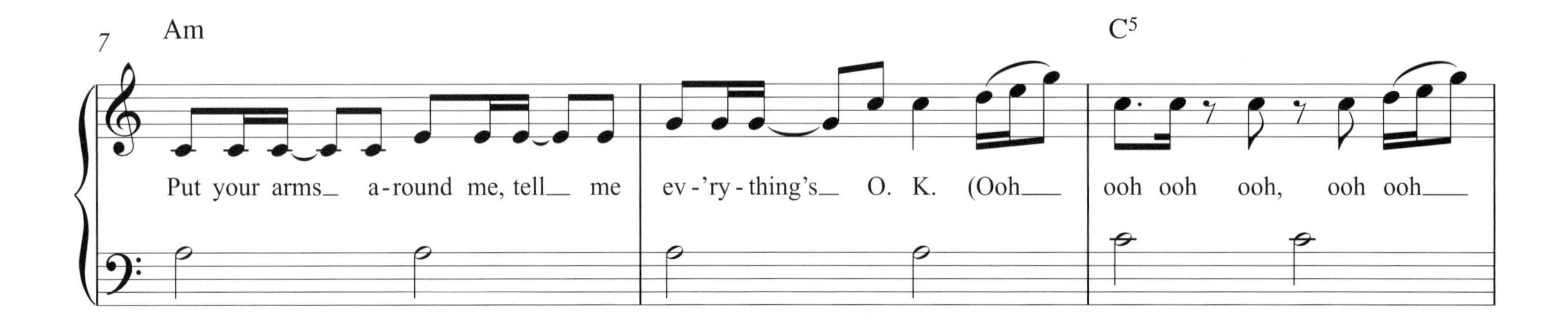
7
Am
C5
Put your arms a-round me, tell me
ev-'ry-thing's O. K. (Ooh
ooh ooh ooh, ooh ooh

10
C5
C5/B
ooh ooh ooh, ooh ooh.)
In my mind I'm run-ning 'round a
cold and emp - ty space. (Ooh

13
Am
C5/F
Just 'put your arms_ a-round me, tell_ me
ooh ooh ooh, ooh ooh___ ooh ooh ooh, ooh ooh.)___
16
C5/G
C5
ev-'ry-thing's_ O. K. (Ooh___ ooh ooh ooh, ooh ooh___ ooh ooh ooh, ooh ooh.)___
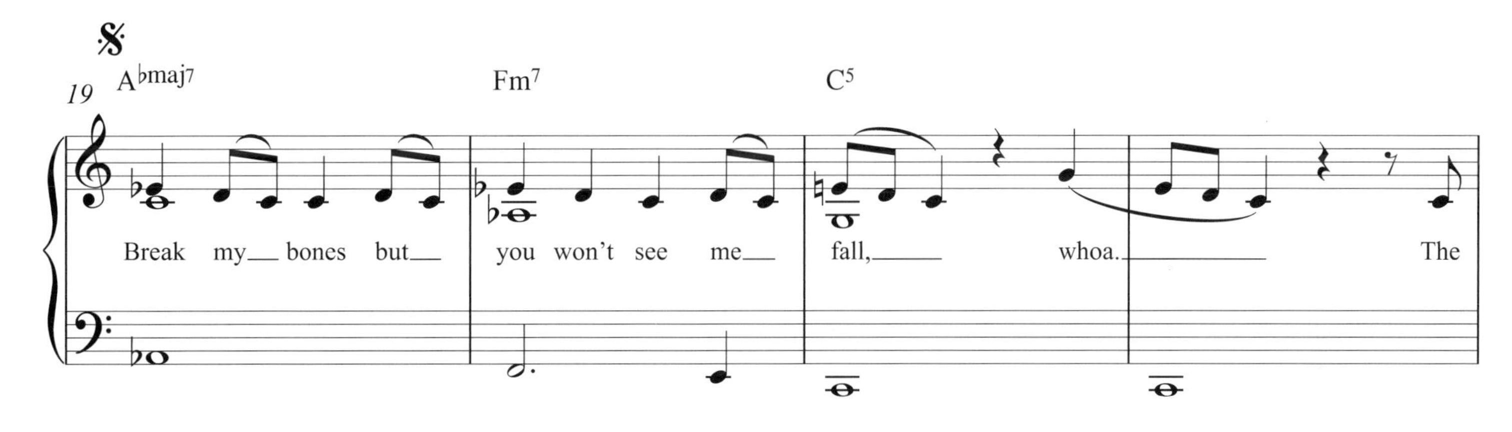
19
A♭maj7
Fm7
C5
Break my_ bones but_ you won't see me_ fall,___ whoa.___ The
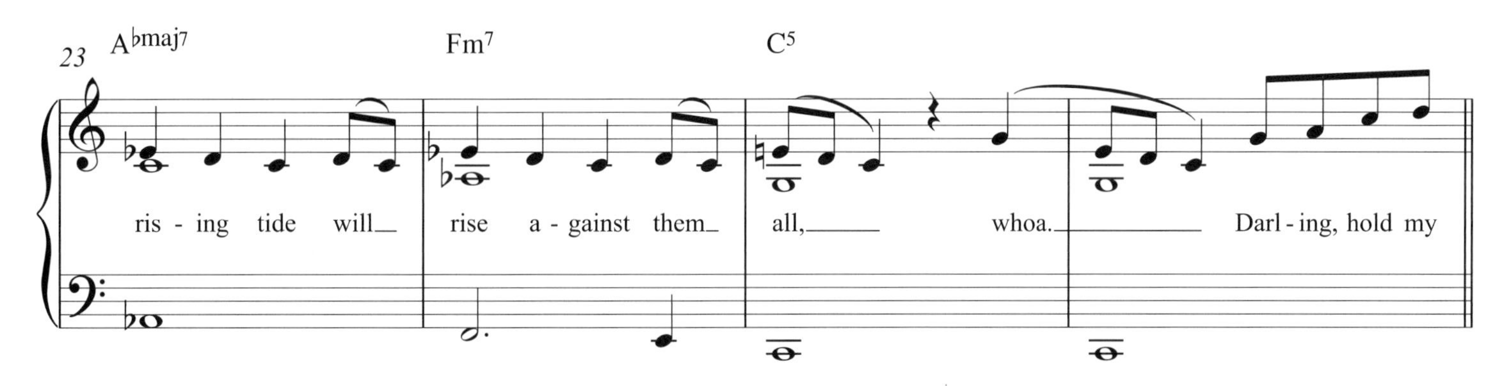
23
A♭maj7
Fm7
C5
ris-ing tide will_ rise a-gainst them_ all,___ whoa.___ Darl-ing, hold my

27
Cmaj9
Em7
hand.___ Oh, won't you hold my hand?___

30
F
'Cause I don't wan - na
walk on my own an - y -
32 Am/E
Dm7
- more won't you un - der - stand?
'Cause
I don't wan-na walk a-lone.
35 C
C/B
I'm read - y for this, there's
no de - ny - ing.
37 Am
F
I'm read-y for this, you
stop me fall - ing.
I'm read-y for this, I
40 F/E
Dm7
To Coda
G
need you all in.
I'm read-y for this, so
darl-ing, hold my hand.

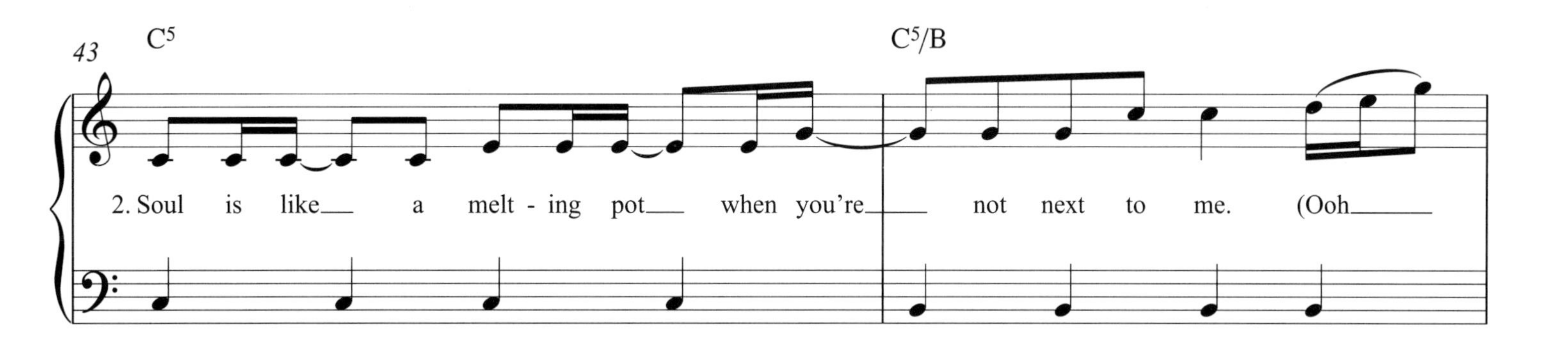
43
C5
C5/B
2. Soul is like a melt - ing pot when you're not next to me. (Ooh

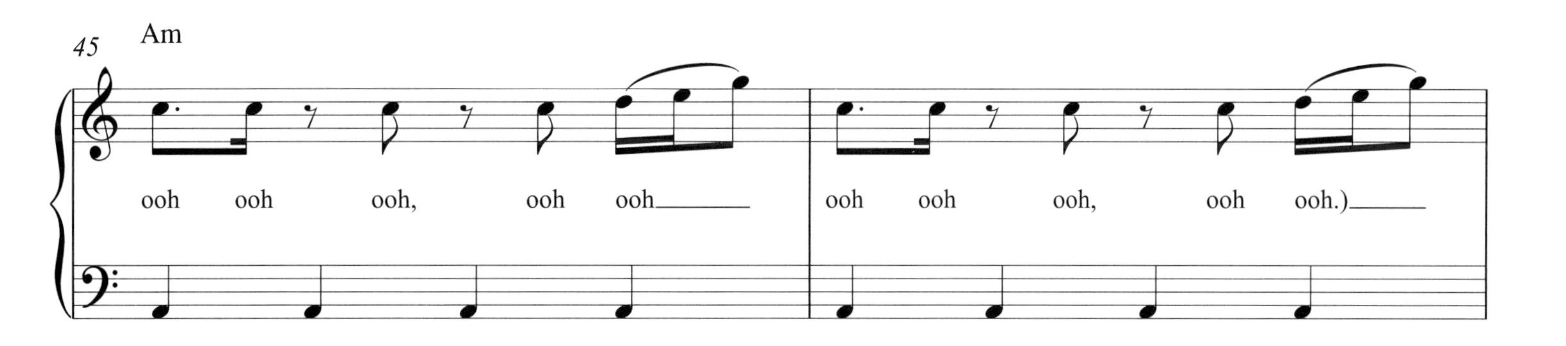
45
Am
ooh ooh ooh, ooh ooh
ooh ooh ooh, ooh ooh.)

47
C5/F
C5/G
Tell me that you got me and you're nev - er gon - na leave. (Ooh

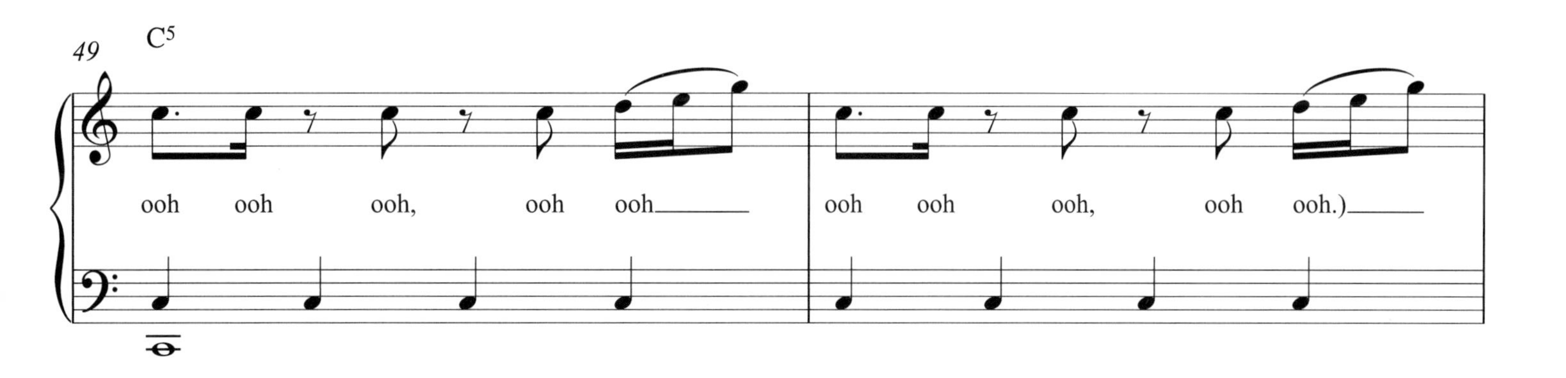
49
C5
ooh ooh ooh, ooh ooh
ooh ooh ooh, ooh ooh.)

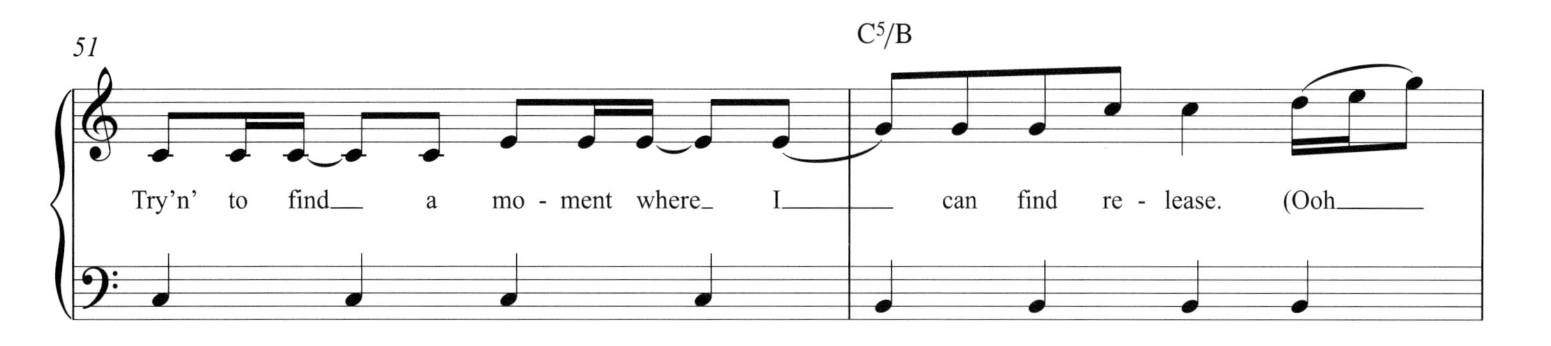
51
C5/B
Try'n' to find a mo - ment where I can find re - lease. (Ooh

53
Am
ooh ooh ooh, ooh ooh
Please
ooh ooh ooh, ooh ooh.)
55
C5/F
C5/G
tell me that you got me and you're
nev - er gon - na leave. (Ooh
57
C5
D.S. al Coda
ooh ooh ooh, ooh ooh
ooh ooh ooh, ooh ooh.)
Coda
59
G
Fmaj7
darl - ing, hold my hand. Don't
wan - na know
that feel - ing when I'm
62
Am
Fmaj7
Em7
all a - lone.
So please don't make me
wait, 'cause I don't wan - na

65
Dm7
C
G
break, no, I don't wan - na
fall.
When you're
68
Fmaj7
Am
next to me,
can tell I'm not a -
fraid to be,
71
Fmaj7
Em7
Dm7
C
that you don't make me
wait and nev - er let me
break, you nev - er let me
74
G
Cmaj9
fall.
Darl - ing, hold my
hand.
77
Em7
Oh, won't you hold my
hand?
'Cause I don't wan - na

80
Dm7
walk on my own an - y -
Em7
more, won't you un - der - stand?
82
F
'Cause
N.C.
I don't wan-na walk a - lone.
C
I'm read-y for this, there's
85
C/B
no de - ny - ing.
Am
I'm read-y for this, you
stop me fall - ing.
88
F
I'm read - y for this, I
F/E
need you all in.
90
Dm7
I'm read - y for this, so
G
darl - ing, won't you hold my hand?

I Really Like You

Words & Music by Peter Svensson, Carly Rae Jepsen & Jacob Hindlin

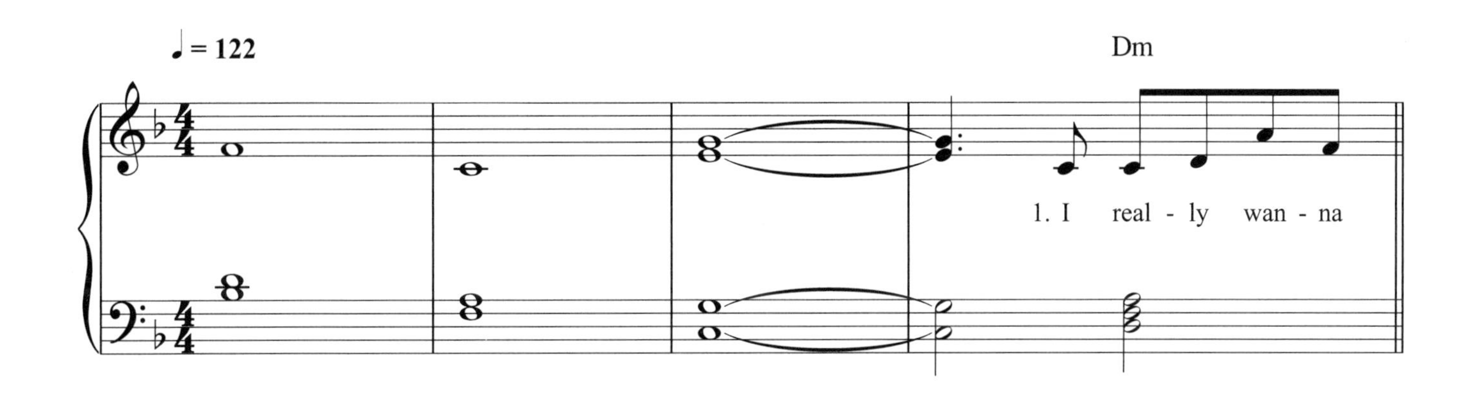

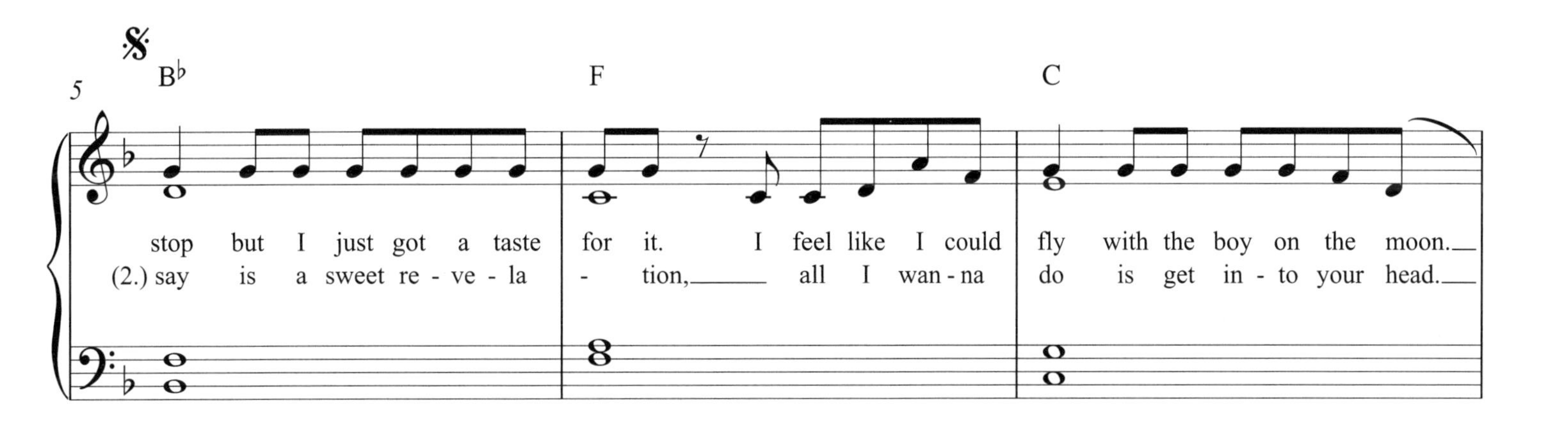

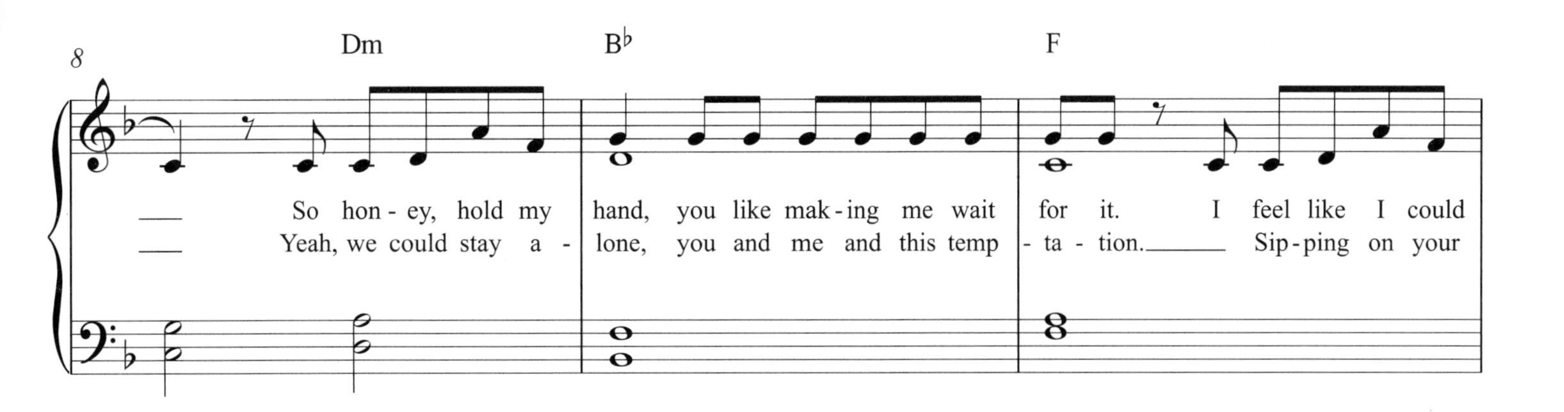

11
C
Dm
B♭
die walk-ing up to the room. (Oh, yeah.)
lips, hang-ing on by a thread. (Ba - by.)
Late night watch-ing
14
F
C
Dm
B♭
te - le-vi - sion but how'd we get in this po-si - tion? It's way too soon, I
18
F
C
N.C.
know this is - n't love but I need to tell you some-thing:
21
B♭
F
C
I real-ly, real-ly, real-ly, real-ly, real-ly, real-ly like you. And I want you, do you
24
Dm
B♭
F
want me, do you want me too? I real-ly, real-ly, real-ly, real-ly, real-ly, real-ly like you.

27
C
Dm
B♭
And I want you, do you want me, do you want me too?
Oh, did I say
30
F
C
Dm
too much? I'm so in my head when we're out - ta touch. (Out - ta touch!)
33
B♭
F
C
I real - ly, real - ly, real - ly, real - ly, real - ly, real - ly like you. And I want you, do you
To Coda
D.S. al Coda
36
Dm
N.C.
want me, do you want me too? 2. It's like ev - 'ry thing you
Coda
38
B♭
F
Who gave you eyes like that, said you could keep them?

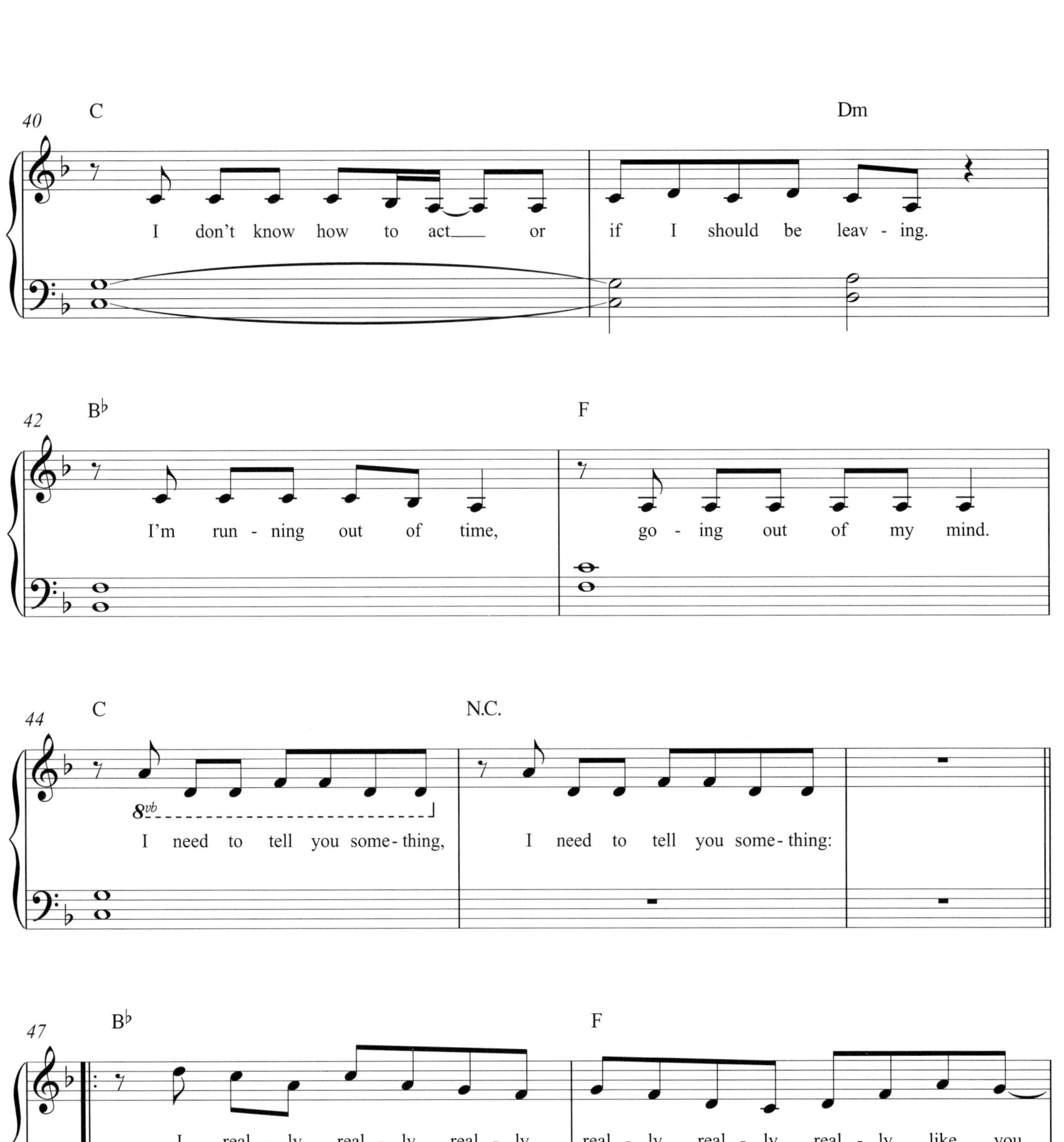
40
C
Dm
I don't know how to act___ or
if I should be leav - ing.
42
B♭
F
I'm run - ning out of time,
go - ing out of my mind.
44
C
N.C.
8vb
I need to tell you some - thing,
I need to tell you some - thing:

47
B♭
F
I real - ly, real - ly, real - ly,
real - ly, real - ly, real - ly like you.___
49
C
Dm
___ And I want you, do you
want me, do you want me too?

51
B♭
F
I real - ly, real - ly, real - ly,
real - ly, real - ly, real - ly like you.
53
C
1.
Dm
And I want you, do you
want me, do you want me too?
55
B♭
F
C
Oh, did I say
too much? I'm so in
my head when we're out -
58
Dm
B♭
F
- ta touch. (Out - ta touch!)
I real - ly, real - ly, real - ly,
real - ly, real - ly, real - ly like you.
61
C
Dm
2.
Dm
And I want you, do you
want me, do you want me too?
want me, do you want me too?

King

Words & Music by Andrew Smith, Oliver Thornton,
Michael Goldsworthy, Resul Turkmen & Mark Ralph

15
Bm A Em D Bm A
try.
price?
Cut co - ver, take that test.
18
Em D Bm A
Hold cou - rage to your chest.
Don't want to wait for you.
20
Em D Bm A Em D
Don't want to have to lose
all that I've com - prom - ised
to feel an - oth - er high,
23
Bm A Em D Bm A
I've got to keep it down to - night.
And
oh,
26
Em D Bm A Em D
I was a king
un - der your con - trol.
And

29
Bm A Em D Bm A
oh, I wan - na feel like you've let me go,
1, 3.
32
Em D Bm A Em D
so let me go.
To Coda
2.
35
Bm A Em D Em D
38
G/D D G A G/D D
I had to break my-self to car - ry on.
No love and no ad - mis - sion,
41
G A Em D G A Em D
take this from me to-night.
Oh, let's fight.

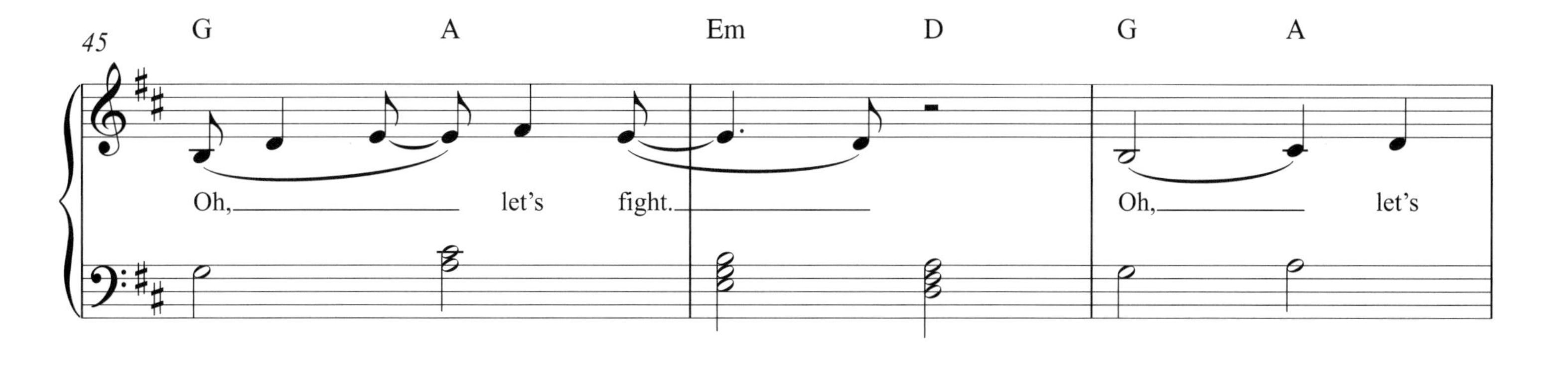
45
G A Em D G A
Oh, let's fight. Oh, let's

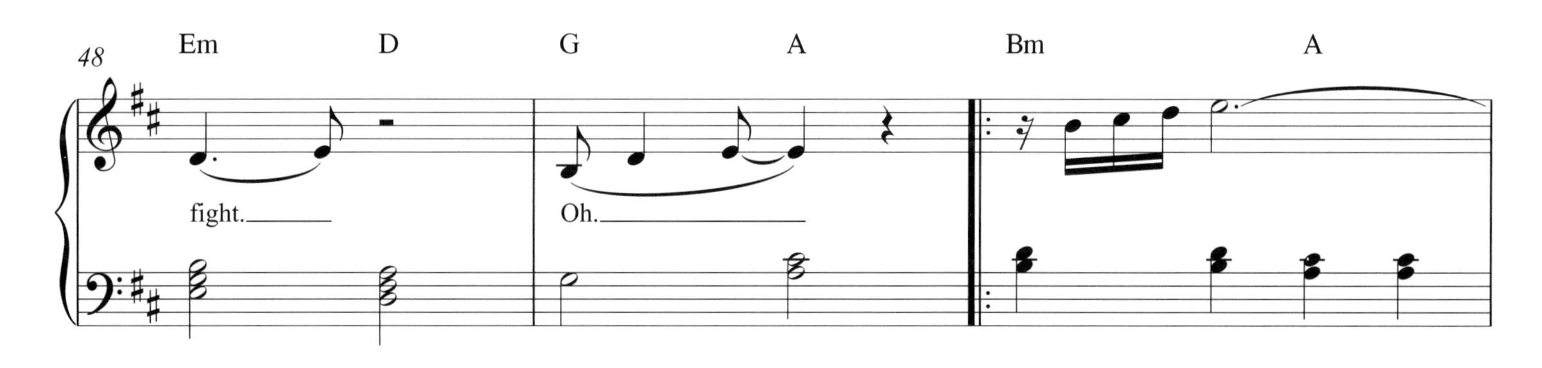
48
Em D G A Bm A
fight. Oh.

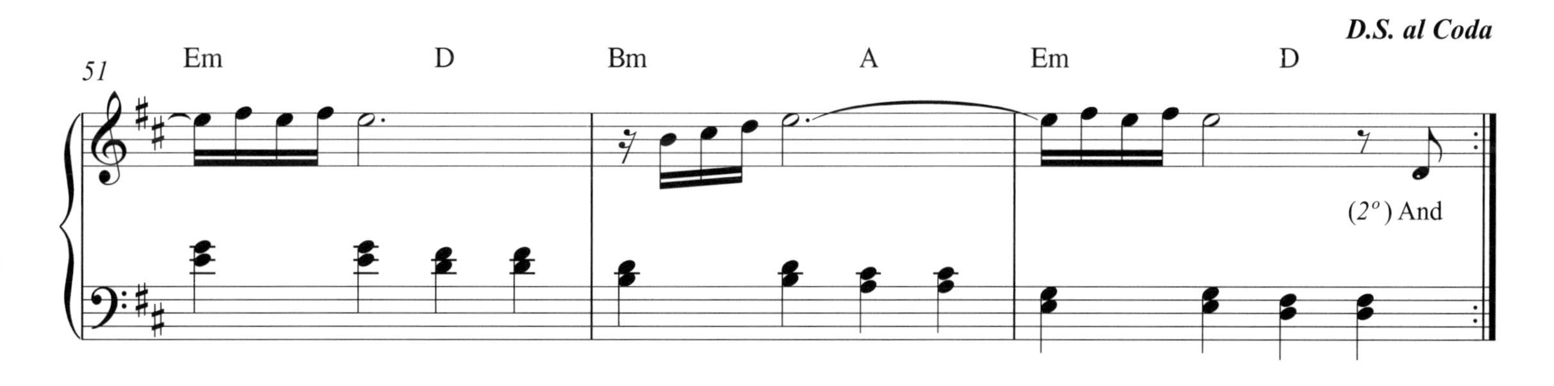
D.S. al Coda
51
Em D Bm A Em D
(2º) And

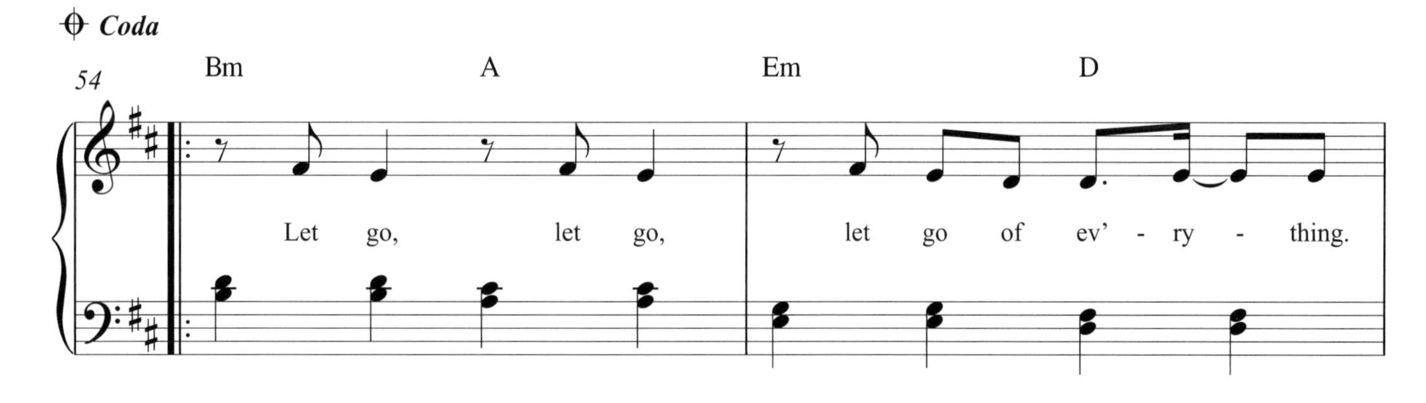
Coda
54
Bm A Em D
Let go, let go, let go of ev' - ry - thing.

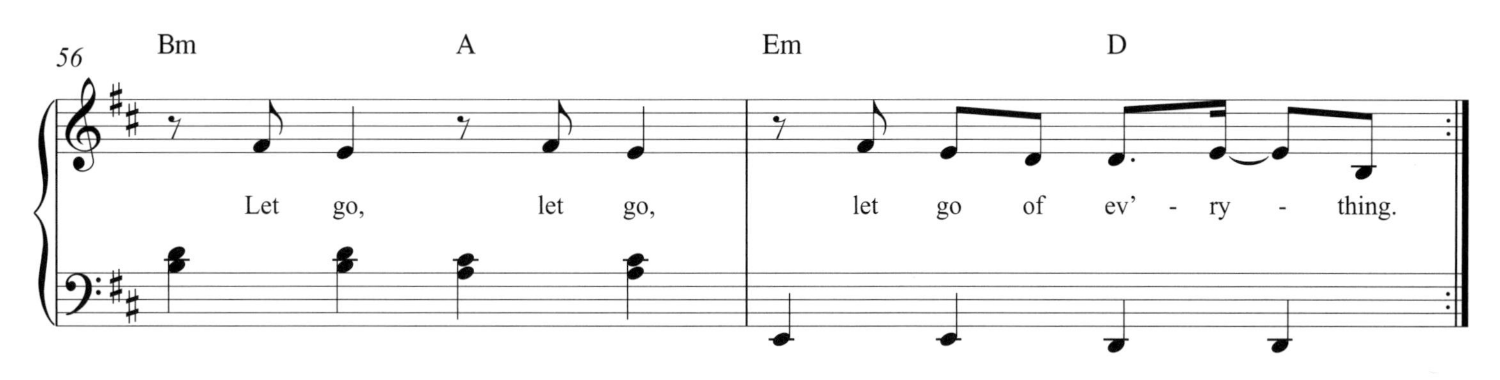
56
Bm A Em D
Let go, let go, let go of ev' - ry - thing.

Lay Me Down

Words & Music by James Napier, Sam Smith & Elvin Smith

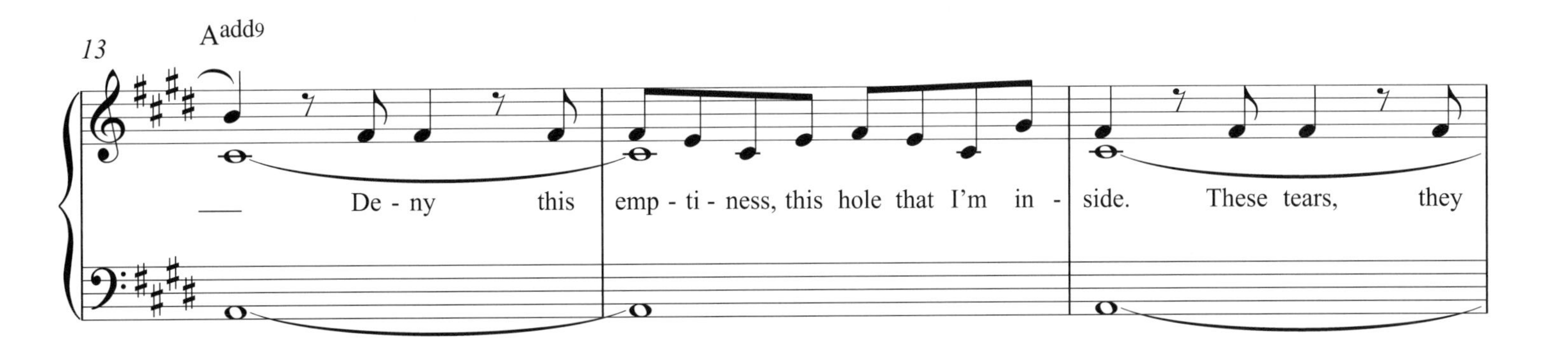
13
Aadd9
De - ny this emp - ti - ness, this hole that I'm in - side. These tears, they

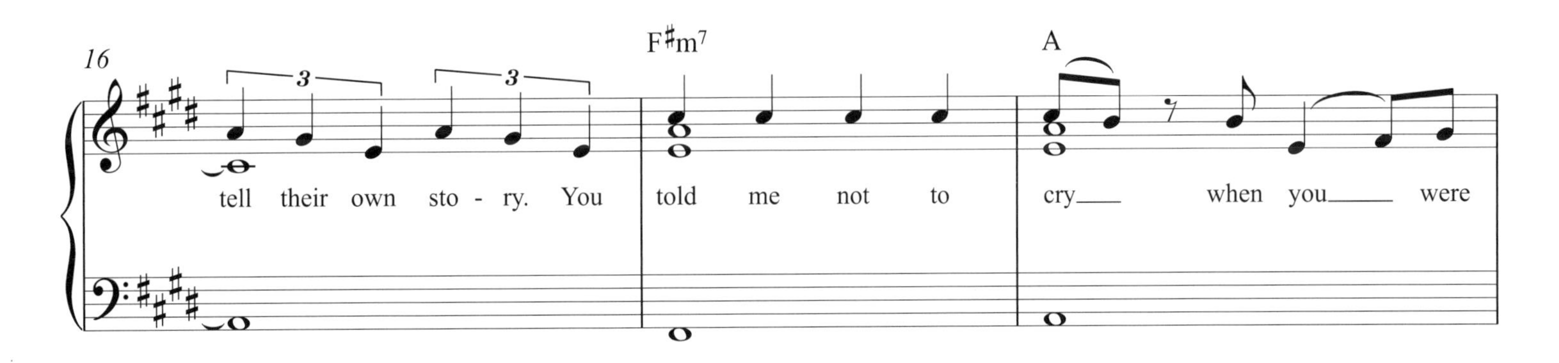
16
F♯m7
A
tell their own sto - ry. You told me not to cry when you were

19
C♯m7
Badd9
F♯m7
gone. But the feel - ing's o - ver -

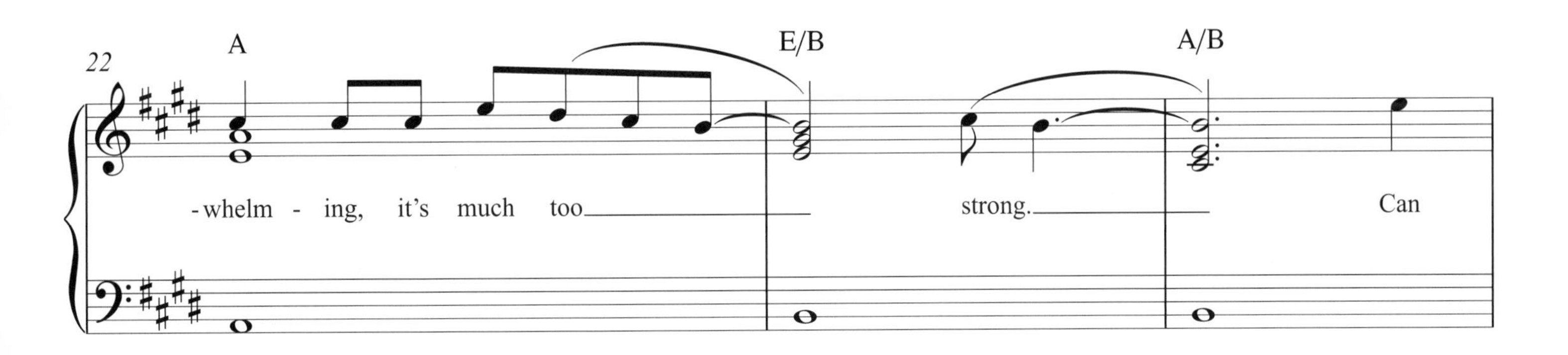
22
A
E/B
A/B
-whelm - ing, it's much too strong. Can

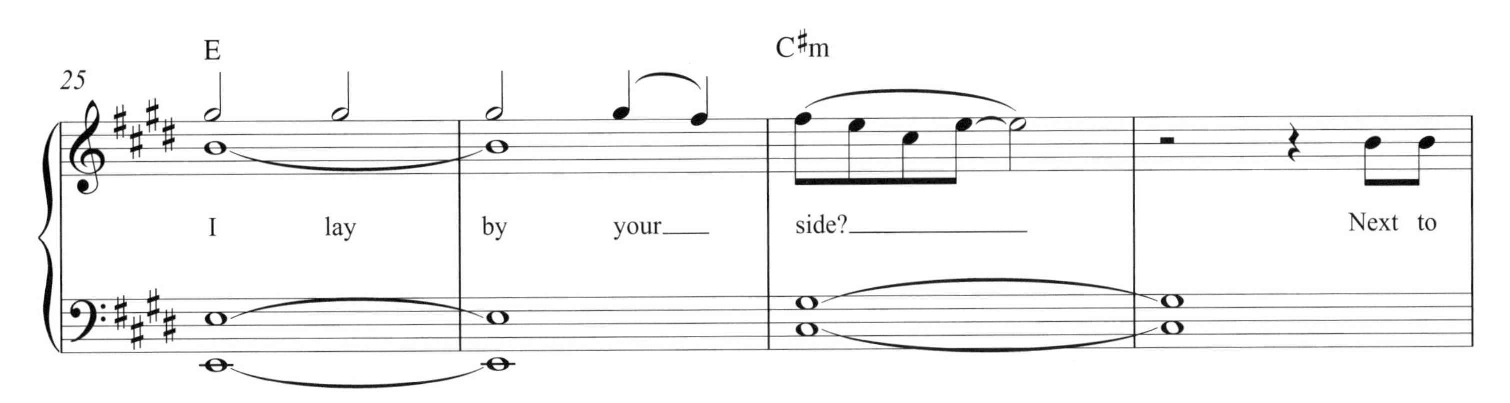
25
E
C♯m
I lay by your side? Next to

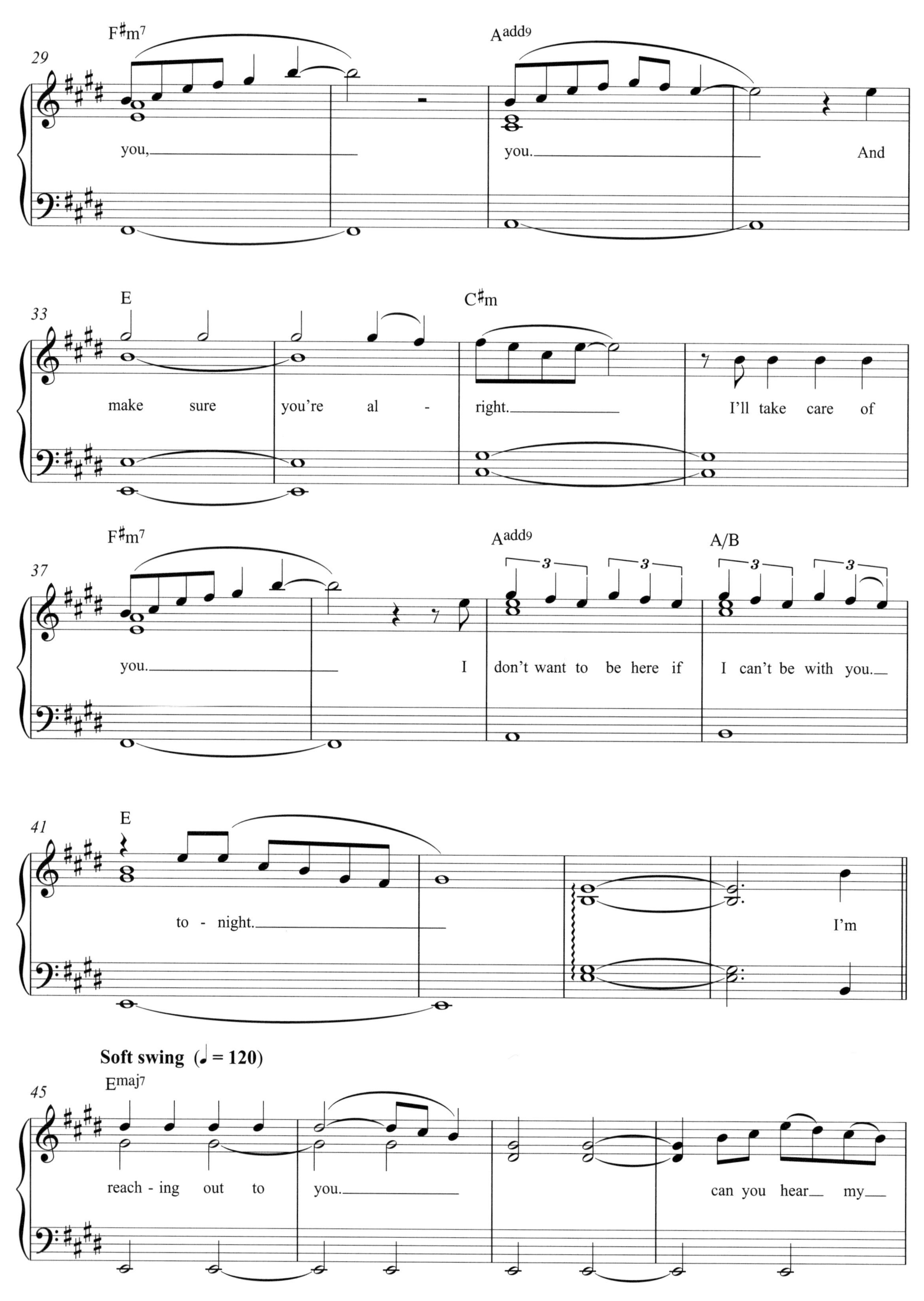

F♯m7
Aadd9
29
you,
you.
And
E
C♯m
33
make sure you're al - right.
I'll take care of
F♯m7
Aadd9
A/B
37
you.
I don't want to be here if
I can't be with you.
41
E
to - night.
I'm
Soft swing (♩ = 120)
Emaj7
45
reach - ing out to you.
can you hear my

49
Aadd9
call?
(Who's to say you won't hear me?)
This
53
Emaj7
hurt that I've been through.
I'm miss-ing you, miss-ing you like
57
Aadd9
E/G♯
cra - zy,
yeah yeah, oh.
You
61
F♯m7
A
C♯m7
Badd9
told me not to cry when you were gone.
But the
65
F♯m7
A
E/B
A/B
feel - ing's o - ver - whelm - ing, it's much too strong.
Can

E
C♯m
69
I lay by your side?
Next to
F♯m7
Aadd9
73
you,
you.
And
E
C♯m
77
make sure you're al - right.
I'll take care of
F♯m7
Aadd9
81
you.
I
don't want to be here if
I can't be with you.
F♯m
F♯m/A
B7sus2
85
to - night.

89
F♯m
F♯m/A
Dmaj7
Lay me down to - night,
92
B7sus2
F♯m
F♯m/A
lay me by your
1.
2.
95
Dmaj7
B7sus2
A/B
(straight quavers)
side.
side.
Can
poco rubato
99
E
C♯m7
I lay by your side?
Next to
rit.
103
F♯m7
Aadd9
Eadd9
you,
you.

See You Again

Words & Music by Justin Franks, Cameron Thomaz,
Charlie Puth & Andrew Cedar

13
E♭
B♭
Gm
B♭
F
see you a - gain.
Damn, who knew? All the
15
E♭
B♭
F
Gm
B♭
F
planes we flew, good things we've been through, that
I'd be stand-ing right here talk-ing to you 'bout an-
17
E♭
B♭
F
Gm
B♭
F
-oth-er path. I know we loved to hit the road and laugh,
but some-thing told me that it would-n't last. Had to
19
E♭
B♭
F
Gm
B♭
F
switch up, look at things diff-'rent see the big-ger pic-ture.
Those were the days. Hard work for-ev - er pays.
21
E♭
B♭
Gm
B♭
F
Now I see you in a bet-ter place.
Uh.
How can we not

23
E♭ B♭ F Gm B♭ F
talk a-bout fam-'ly when fam-'ly's all that we got? Ev -'ry-thing I went through, you were stand-ing there by my side, and
25
E♭ B♭ Gm B♭
now you gon' be with me for the last ride.
It's been a long day with-
27
E♭ B♭ Gm B♭ E♭ B♭ F
-out you my friend, and I'll tell you all a - bout it when I see you a - gain. We've come a
(Spoken:) I see you again.
30
Gm B♭ E♭ B♭ Gm B♭
long way from where we be - gan, oh, I'll tell you all a - bout it when I
Yeah, we came a long way. You know where we started.
33
E♭ B♭ E♭ B♭
see you a - gain, when I see you a - gain. (Oh.
Gonna tell you.

Gm
B♭
F
E♭
B♭
F
Gm
B♭
F
35
Oh.
Ooh.
E♭
B♭
Gm
B♭
F
38
First you both
E♭
B♭
F
40
go out your way and the vibe is feel - ing strong, that what's small
Gm
B♭
F
41
turn to a friend - ship, a friend - ship turn to a bond, and that bond -
E♭
B♭
F
Gm
B♭
F
42
-'ll nev - er be bro - ken, the love will nev - er get lost.
And when broth -

44
E♭
B♭
F
-er - hood comes first, then the line will nev - er be crossed. Est - ab -
45
Gm
B♭
F
-lished it on our own when that line had to be drawn, and that line
46
E♭
B♭
is what we reach, so re - mem - ber me when I'm gone.
47
Gm
B♭
F
E♭
B♭
F
How can we not talk a - bout fam-'ly when fam-'ly's all that we got? Ev-
49
Gm
B♭
F
-'ry - thing I went through, you were stand - ing there by my side, and

50
E♭ B♭ Cm B♭
now you gon' be with me for the last ride.
So let the light guide your way,
52
F Cm B♭ F Gm7
yeah. Hold ev-'ry mem-'ry as you go. And ev-'ry
55
Cm B♭ B♭ F/A Gm F E♭
D.S. al Coda
road you take will al-ways lead you home. Home. It's been a
Coda
59
E♭ B♭ Gm B♭ F E♭ B♭ F
see you a-gain. (Oh. Oh. Ooh.)
62
Gm B♭ F
1.
E♭ B♭
2.
E♭ B♭
When I see you a-gain. (Oh. see you a-gain.

Take Me To Church

Words & Music by Andrew Hozier-Byrne

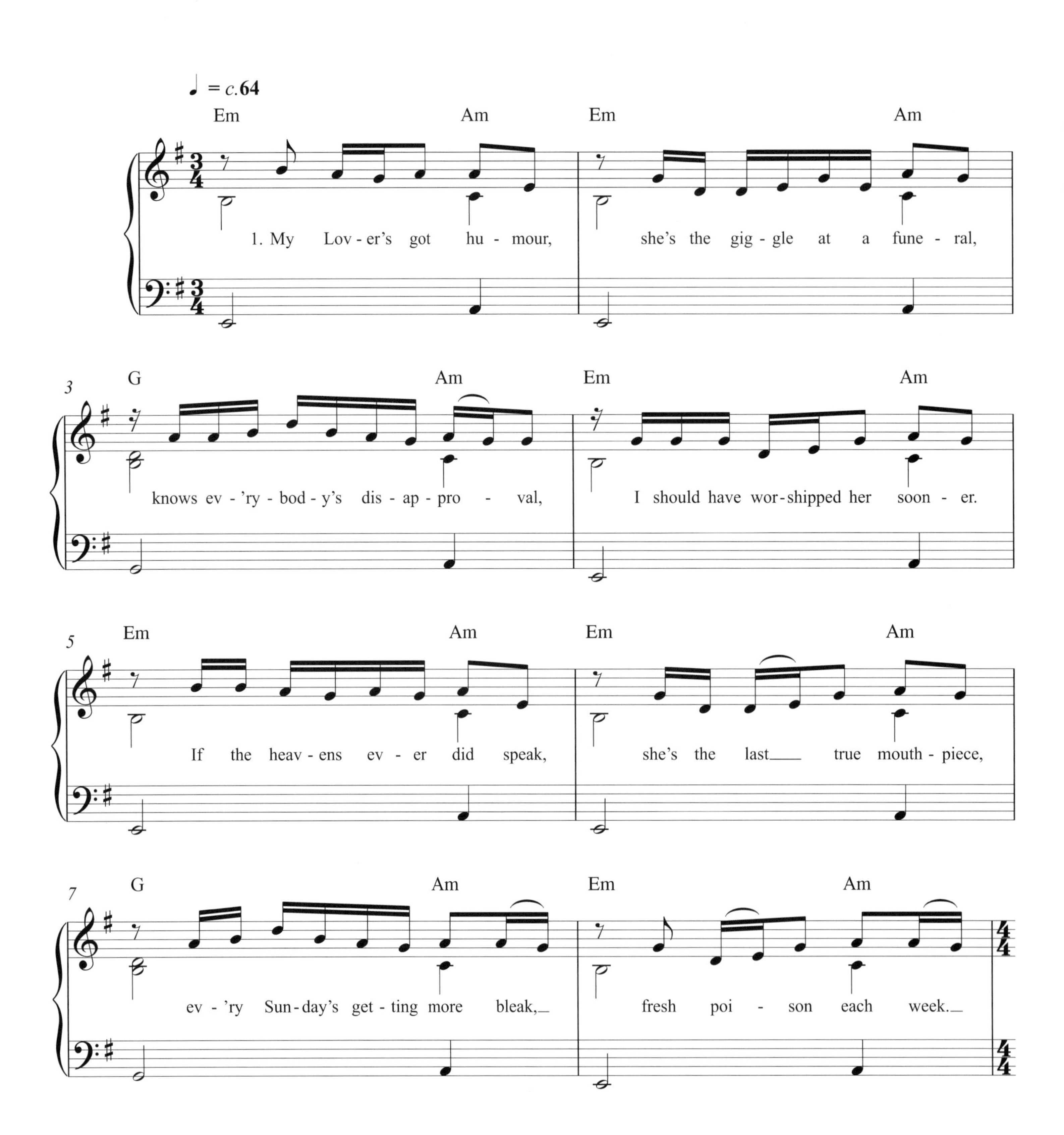

D
C
Em
Am
We were born_ sick, you heard them say it.
My Church of-fers no_ ab-so-lutes,
Em
Am
G
Am
she tells me, "Wor-ship in the bed-room,"
the on-ly heav-en I'll be sent to
Em
Am
D
C
is when I'm a-lone with you.
I was born_ sick, but I love_ it,
C
G
C
com-mand me to be well. A,_ a-
G
Cm
G
Cm
G
-men, a-men,_ a-men._ Take me to Church,_

Slight shuffle
20
Em
B
I'll wor-ship like a dog at the shrine of your lies,
I'll tell you my sins and you can shar-pen your knife,
22
G
Am
1.
Em
of-fer me that death-less death, oh good God,
let me give you my life.
Take me to Church
2, 3.
24
Em
To Coda
Em
Am
let me give you my life.
If I'm a pa-gan of the good times,
26
Em
Am
G
Am
my lov-er's the sun-light.
To keep the God-dess on my side,
28
G
Am
D
C
she de-mands a sa-cri-fice.
Drain the whole sea, get some-thing shi-ny,

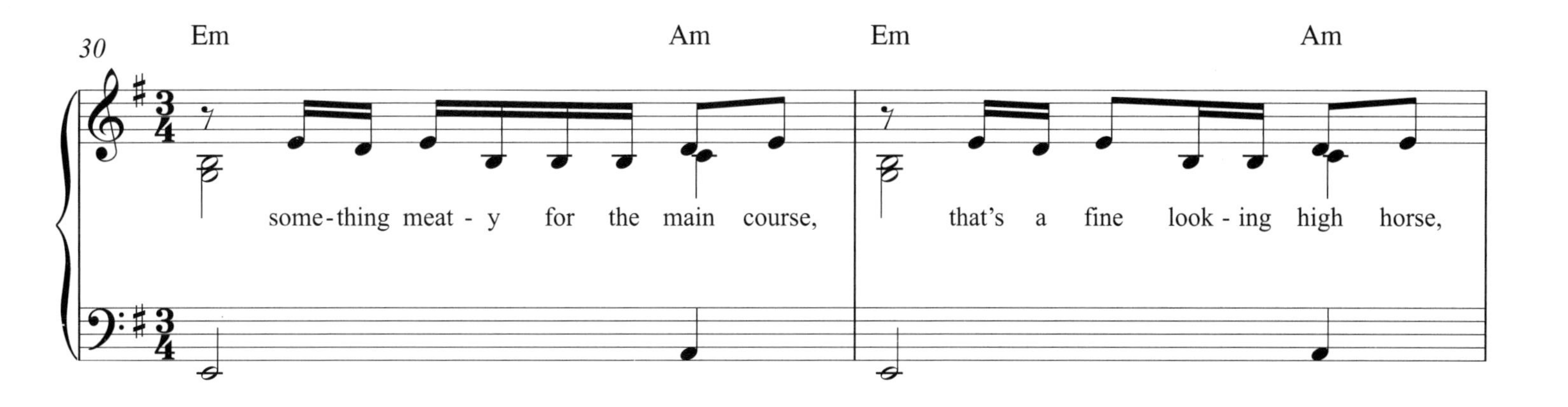
30
Em Am Em Am
some-thing meat - y for the main course,
that's a fine look - ing high horse,

32
G Am Em Am
what you got in the sta - ble?
We've got a lot of starv - ing faith - ful.

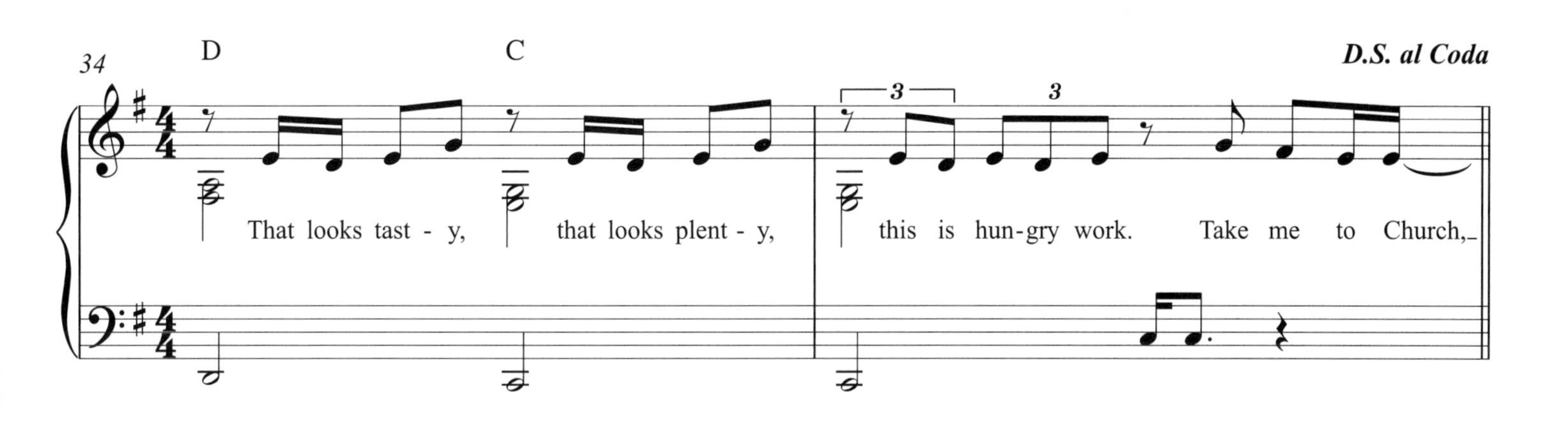
34
D C
D.S. al Coda
That looks tast - y, that looks plent - y,
this is hun-gry work. Take me to Church,

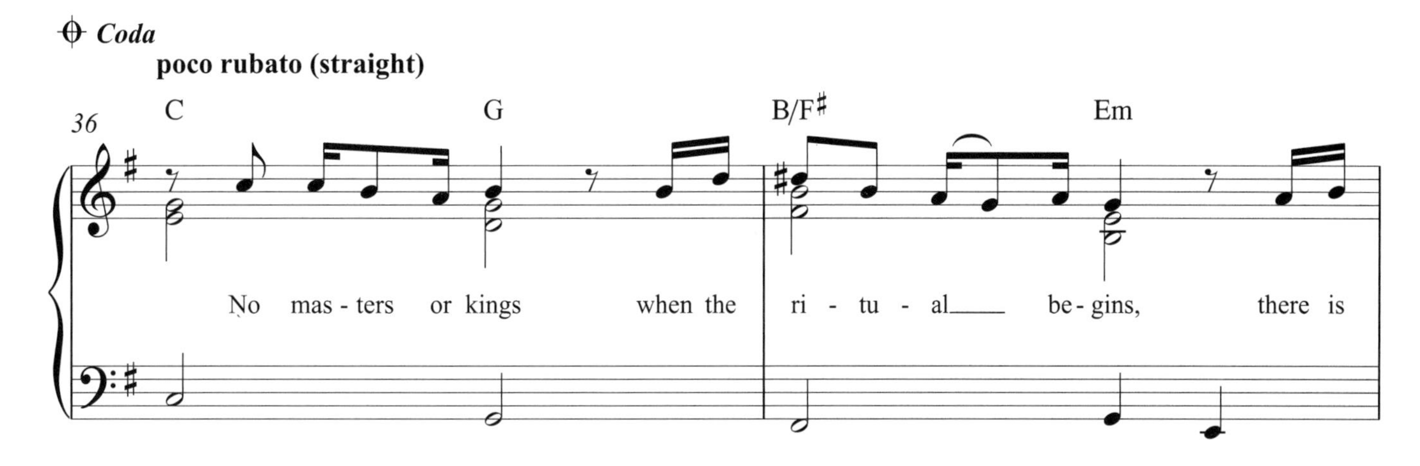
Coda
poco rubato (straight)
36
C G B/F# Em
No mas - ters or kings when the
ri - tu - al begins, there is

C G B/F♯ Em
no sweet - er in - no - cence than our gen - tle sin. In the
C G B/F♯ Em
mad - ness and soil of that sad earth - ly scene, on - ly
C G B/F♯ Em
then I am hu - man, on - ly then I am clean.
Em/D C G C
Oh. Oh. A -
G Cm G Cm G
- men, a - men, a - men. Take me to Church,

Slight shuffle
Em
I'll wor - ship like a dog at the shrine of your lies,
B
I'll tell you my sins and you can shar - pen your knife,
G
Am
of - fer me that death - less death, oh good God,
1.
Em
let me give you my life. Take me to Church
2.
Em
let me give you my life.

Thinking Out Loud

Words & Music by Ed Sheeran & Amy Wadge

9
D D/F♯ G A D D/F♯
will__ be lov-ing you till__ we're se-ven-ty.__
soul__ could nev-er grow old,__ it's ev-er-green.
12
G A D D/F♯
And ba-by, my heart__ could still feel as
And ba-by, your smile's__ for-ev-er in
14
G A D D/F♯ G A
hard__ at twen-ty-three.__ And I'm think-ing 'bout how__
my mind__ and mem-o-ry.__ And I'm think-ing 'bout how__
17
Em A D Em
peo-ple fall in love in mys-ter-i-ous ways,__ may-be just the touch of a hand.__
peo-ple fall in love in mys-ter-i-ous ways,__ may-be it's all part of a plan.__
20
A Em A Bm
__ Well me I fall in love with you ev-'ry sin-gle day.__ And
__ Well I'll just keep on mak-ing the same__ mis-takes,__

23
Em
A
N.C.
I just wan - na tell you I am.
hop - ing that you'll un - der - stand.
So hon - ey now,
That ba - by now,
25
D D/F♯
G A
D D/F♯
take me in - to your lov - ing arms.
28
G A
D D/F♯
Kiss me un - der the light of a thou - sand stars.
30
G A
D D/F♯
G A
Place your head on my beat - ing heart
I'm think - ing out loud may - be
33
To Coda
1.
2.
Bm A G D/F♯
Em7 A D
we found love right where we are.
where we are.

D
D/F♯
G
A
(La, la,
la, la, la, la, la, la, la, la, la, la.)
D.S. al Coda
So ba-by now,
Coda
Em7
Bm
where we are. Ba - by, we found love right
where we are. And we found love right where we are.

Uptown Funk!

Words & Music by Rudy Taylor, Robert Wilson, Lonnie Simmons,
Ronnie Wilson, Mark Ronson, Philip Lawrence, Jeffrey Bhasker,
Peter Hernandez, Charles Wilson, Nicholaus Williams & Devon Gallaspy

♩ = 116
Dm7

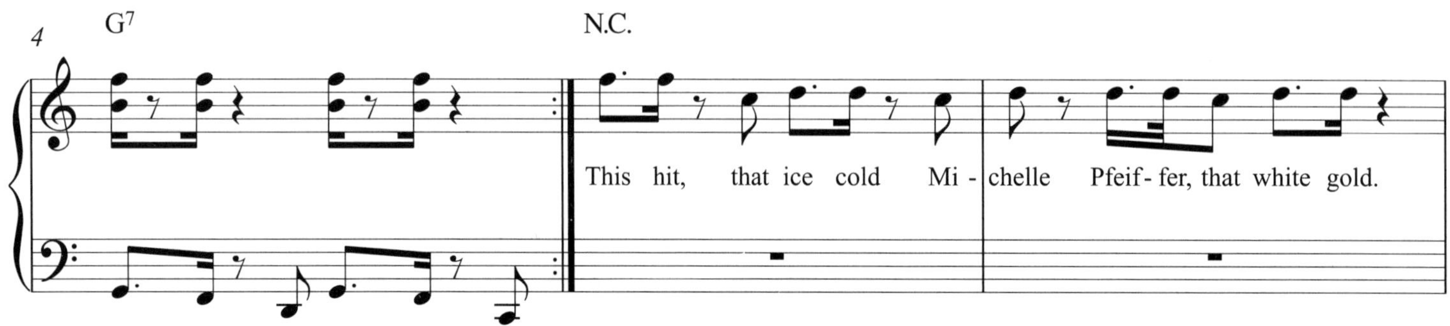
4
G7
N.C.
This hit, that ice cold Mi - chelle Pfeif - fer, that white gold.

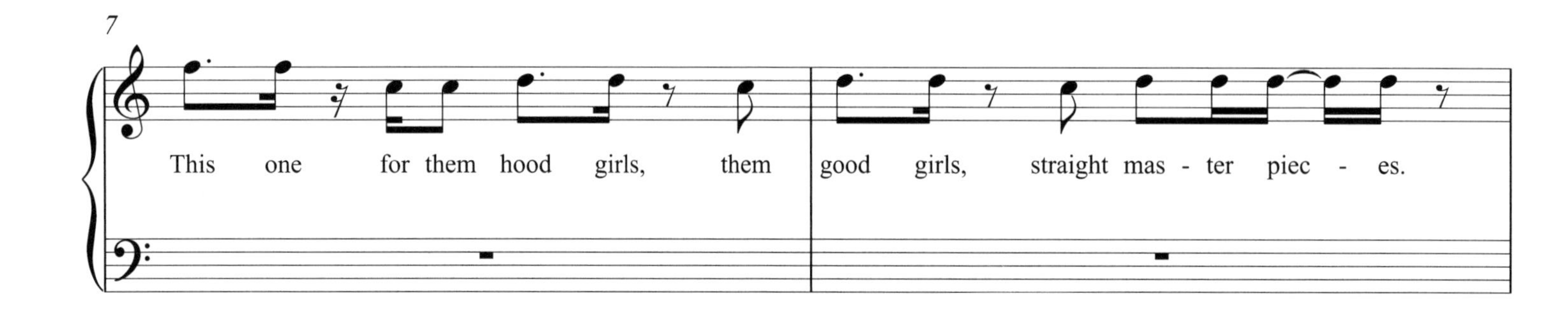
7
This one for them hood girls, them good girls, straight mas - ter piec - es.

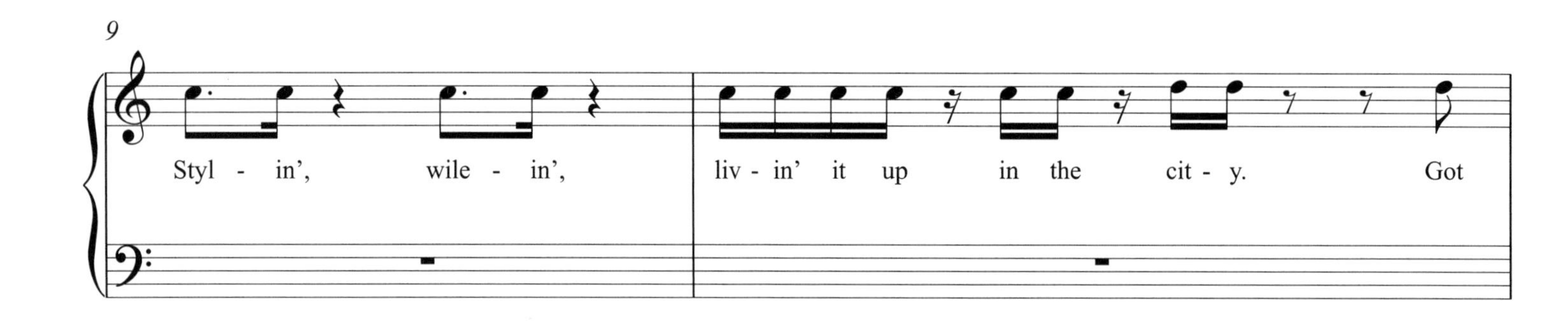
9
Styl - in', wile - in', liv - in' it up in the cit - y. Got

11
Chucks on with Saint Lau-rent. Got to kiss my-self_ I'm so pret-ty. I'm too
13
Dm7
G7
hot, (Hot damn.) called a po - lice and a fire - man. I'm too

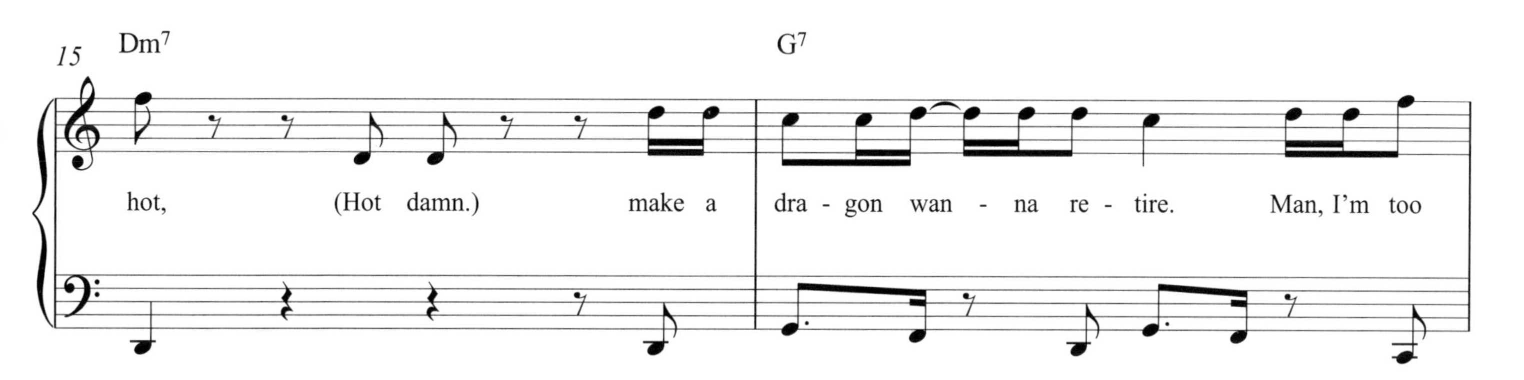
15
Dm7
G7
hot, (Hot damn.) make a dra - gon wan - na re - tire. Man, I'm too

17
Dm7
G7
hot, (Hot damn.) say my name_ you know who I am._ I'm too

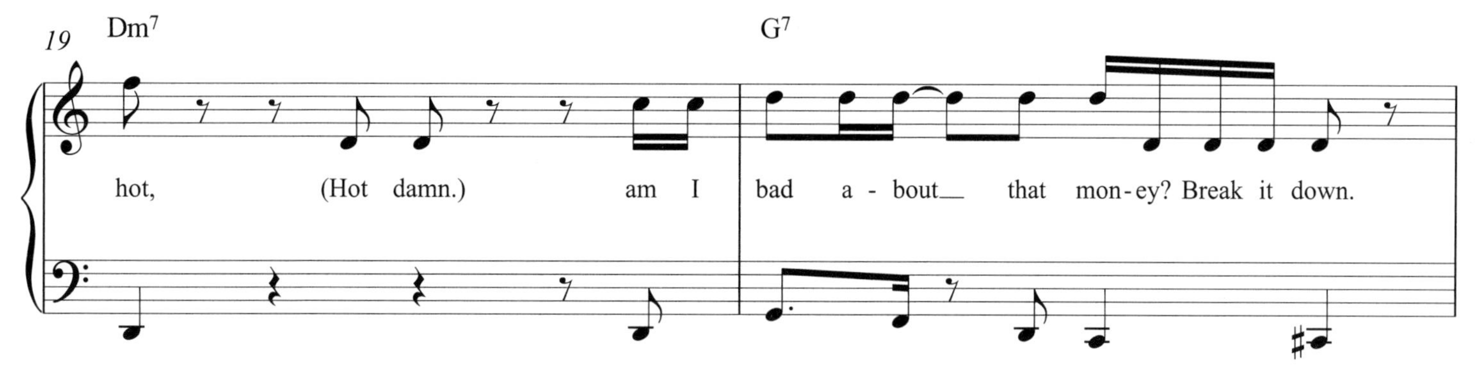
19
Dm7
G7
hot, (Hot damn.) am I bad a - bout_ that mon-ey? Break it down.

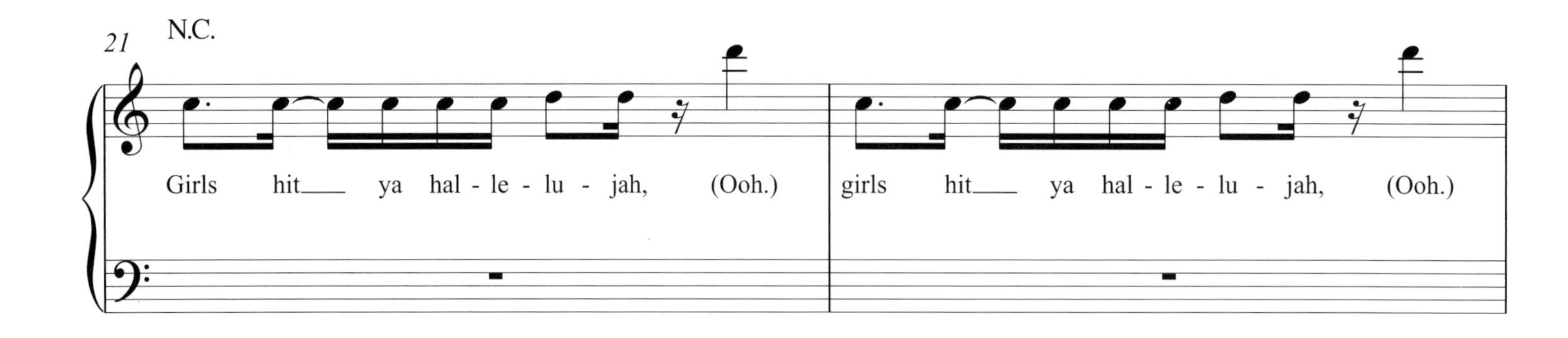
21
N.C.
Girls hit___ ya hal - le - lu - jah, (Ooh.) girls hit___ ya hal - le - lu - jah, (Ooh.)

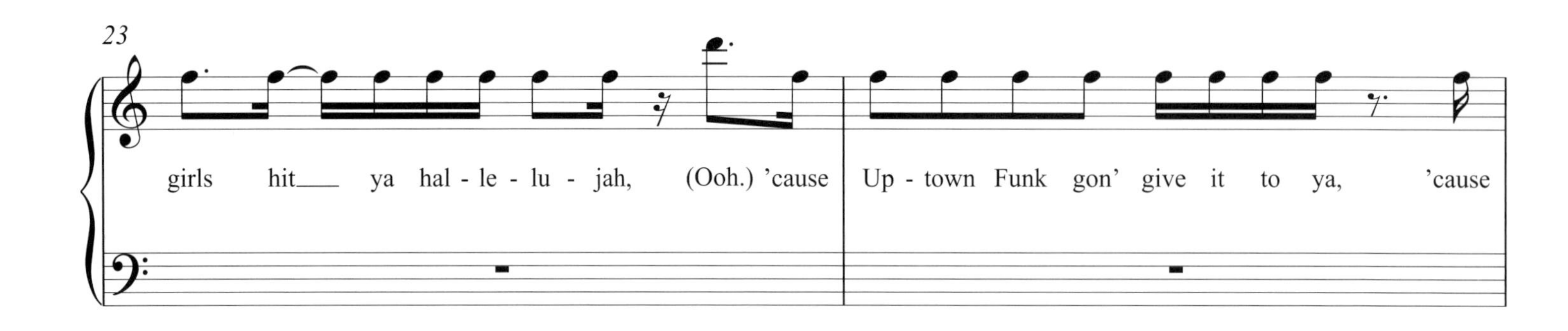
23
girls hit___ ya hal - le - lu - jah, (Ooh.) 'cause Up - town Funk gon' give it to ya, 'cause

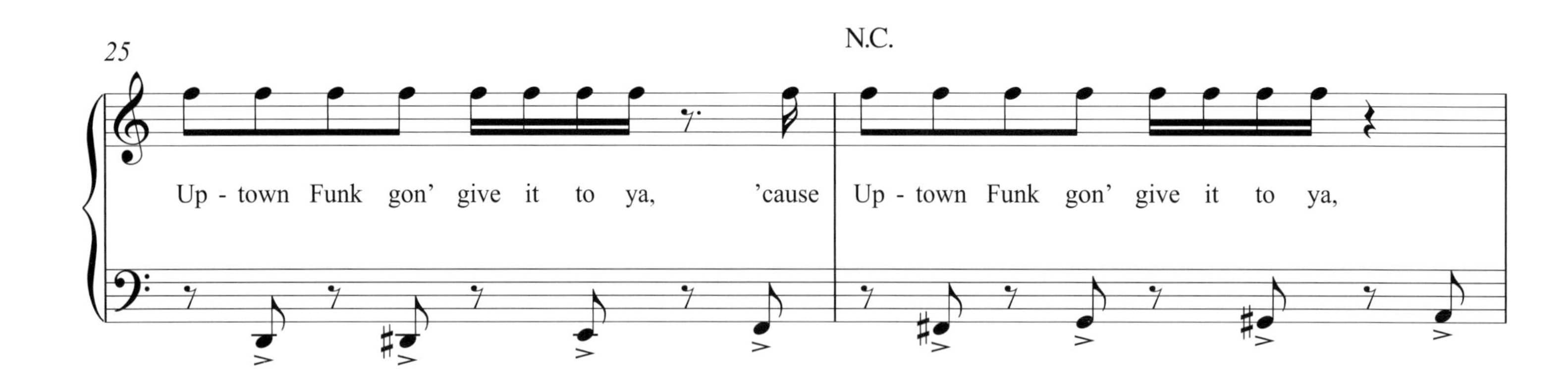
25
N.C.
Up - town Funk gon' give it to ya, 'cause Up - town Funk gon' give it to ya,

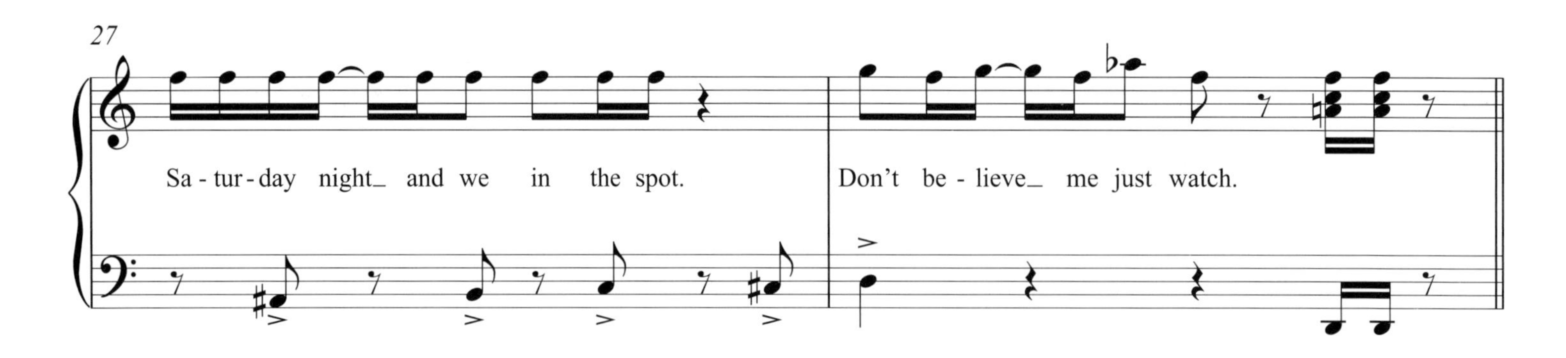
27
Sa - tur - day night_ and we in the spot. Don't be - lieve_ me just watch.

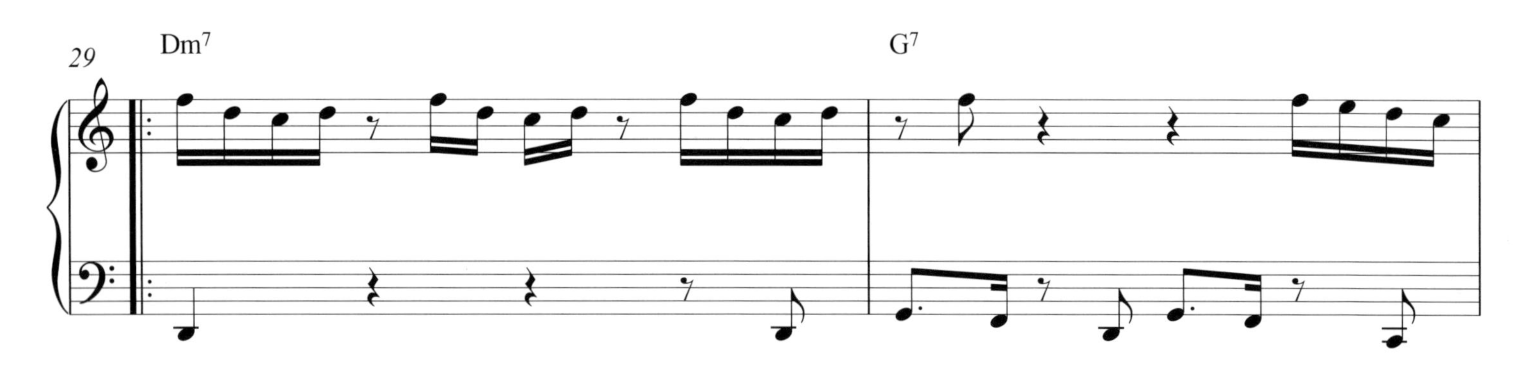
29
Dm7
G7

31
Dm7
G7
Don't be - lieve me just watch.
33
N.C.
Don't be - lieve me just watch.
Don't be - lieve me just watch.
35
To Coda
Don't be - lieve me just watch.
Hey, hey, hey, oh!
37
Dm7
N.C.
Stop. Wait a min - ute.
Fill my cup, put some li - quor in it.
39
Take a sip, sign a cheque.
Ju - li - o! Get the stretch! Ride to

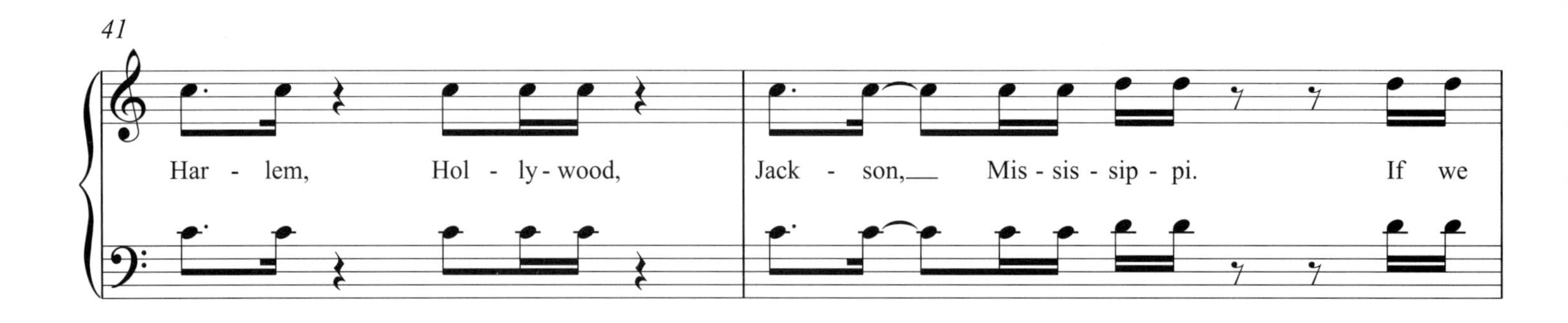
41
Har - lem, Hol - ly - wood, Jack - son, Mis - sis - sip - pi. If we

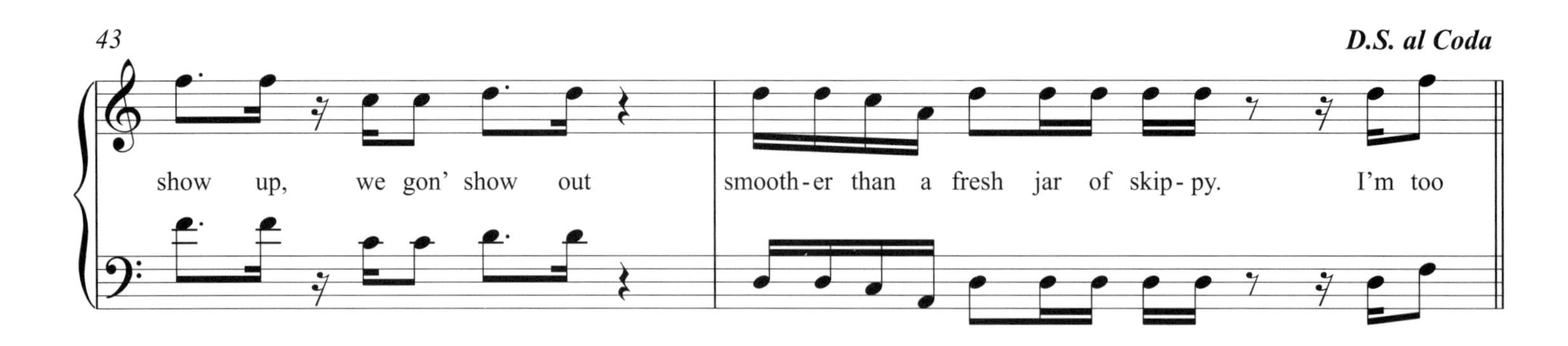
43
D.S. al Coda
show up, we gon' show out smooth - er than a fresh jar of skip - py. I'm too

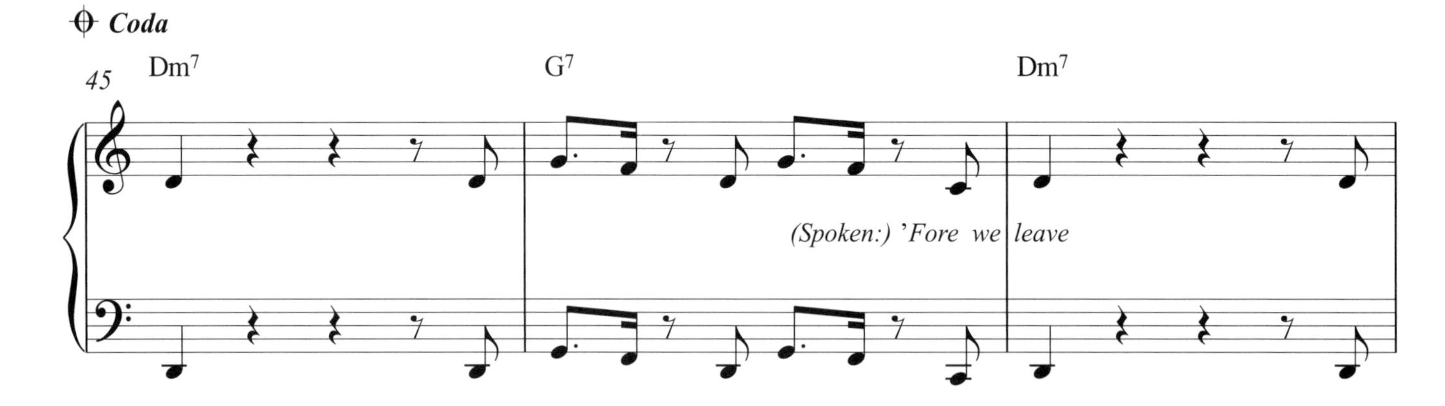
Coda
45
Dm7
G7
Dm7
(Spoken:) 'Fore we leave

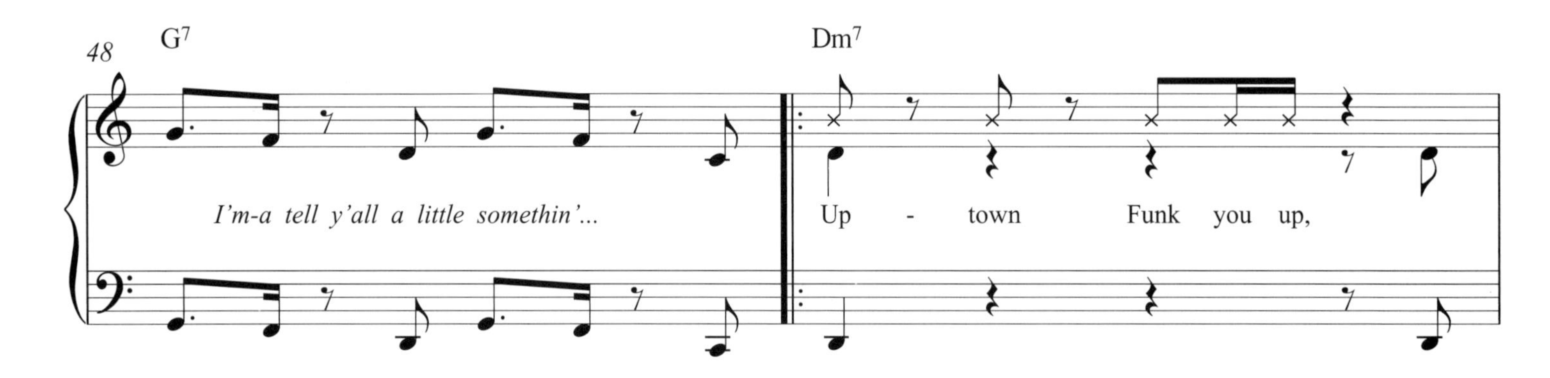
48
G7
Dm7
I'm-a tell y'all a little somethin'...
Up - town Funk you up,

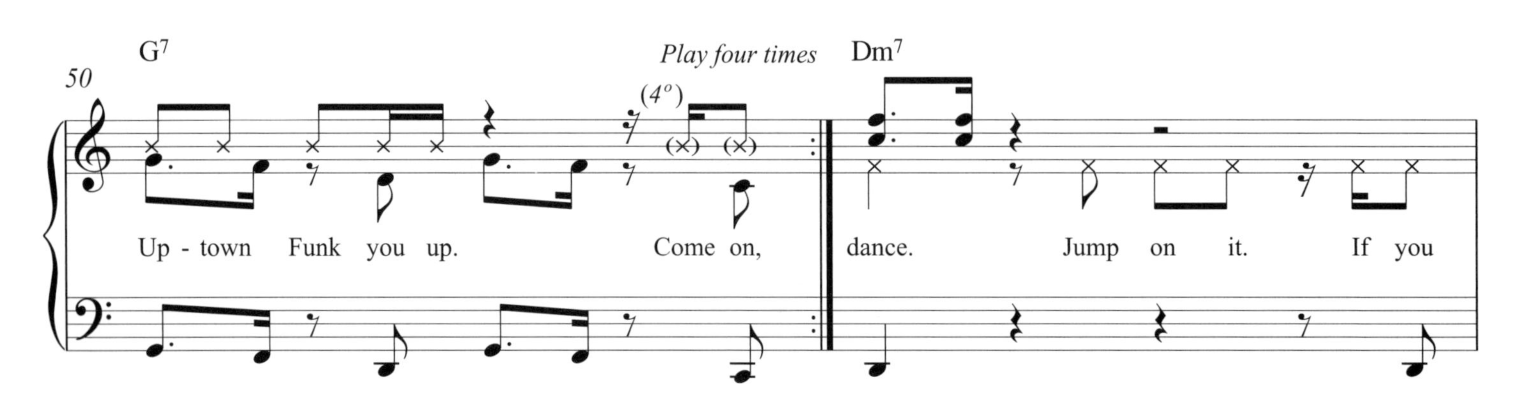
50
G7
Play four times
(4º)
Dm7
Up - town Funk you up. Come on, dance. Jump on it. If you

52
G7
Dm7
sex - y then flaunt it. If you freak - y then own it. Don't
54
G7
Dm7
brag a - bout it just show me. Come on, dance. Jump on it. If you
56
G7
Dm7
sex - y then flaunt it. Well it's Sa - tur - day night and we're in the spot.
58
G7
Dm7
Don't be - lieve me just watch.
60
G7
G7
Don't be - lieve me just watch.

63
N.C.
Don't be - lieve_ me just watch.
Don't be - lieve_ me just watch._
65
Don't be-lieve_ me just watch._
Hey,_ hey, hey, oh!_
Dm7
Up - town Funk you up,
68
G7
Up-town Funk you up.
Dm7
Up - town Funk you up,
G7
Up-town Funk you up.
71
Dm7
Up - town Funk you up,
G7
Up-town Funk you up.
Dm7
Up - town Funk you up,
1.
74
G7
Up - town Funk you up.
2.

Waiting For Love

Words & Music by Simon Aldred, Tim Bergling,
Vincent Pontare, Salem Al Fakir & Martin Garrix

17
C♯
D
E
F♯m
dream-er a dream, we're un-stop-pa-ble, with some - thing to be-lieve in.
love in this life, we're un-stop-pa-ble, no, we can't be de-feat - ed.
21
D
A/C♯
F♯m
Mon - day left me bro-ken, Tues - day I was through with hop-ing, Wednes-day my
25
C♯m7
F♯m/E
Bm
emp - ty arms were o - pen, Thurs - day wait - ing for love,
28
E/G♯
E
wait - ing for love. Thank the stars it's Fri - day, I'm burn-ing like a
31
fire gone wild on Sat-ur-day, guess I won't be com-ing to church on

To Coda
F♯m/E
D A/C♯ Bm F♯m
D A/C♯ Bm E/G♯ E
Sun - day, I'll be wait - ing for love, wait - ing for love to
D
come a - round.
F♯m C♯sus4 D E F♯m
C♯ D Esus2 F♯m
C♯ D E F♯m C♯

54
D
Esus2
F♯m
E
F♯m
C♯sus4
58
D
E
F♯m
C♯
62
D
Esus2
F♯m
D.S. al Coda
2. We are
Coda
65
F♯m
C♯
D
E
F♯m
come a-round.
69
C♯
D
Esus2
F♯m

73
C♯
D
E
F♯m
77
C♯
D
Esus2
F♯m
E
81
F♯m
C♯sus4
D
E
84
F♯m
C♯
D
87
Esus2
F♯m

Wings

Words & Music by Ryan Tedder & Jasmine Van Den Bogaerde

13
C
G
It made me think of you.
It made me think of you.

16
G
2. Un-der a tril-lion stars
we danced on top of cars.
3. I'm in a for-eign state,
my thoughts they slip a-way.

19
Bm
C
Took pic-tures of the stage,
so far from where we are.
They made me think of you,
My words are leav-ing me,
they go an - oth - er place.
Be - cause I thought of you,

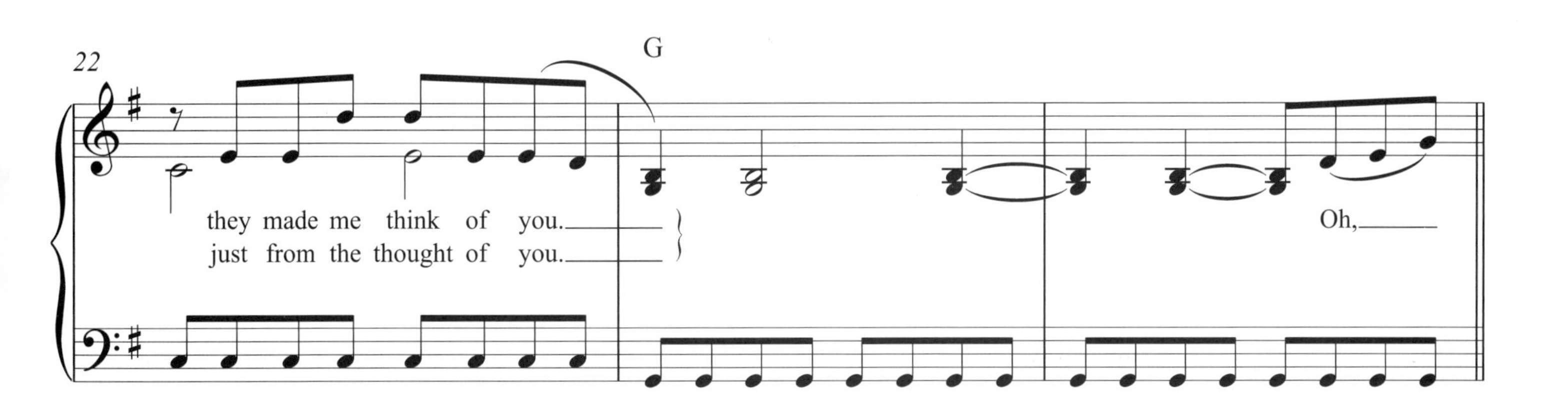
22
G
they made me think of you.
just from the thought of you.
Oh,

25
Em
C
lights go down
in the mo-ment we're
lost and found.
28
Gsus4
G
I just want to be
by your side.
If these wings could fly.
31
D
1.
G
For the rest of our lives.
34
2, 3.
Em
Oh,
damn these walls,
37
C
in the mo-ment we're
ten feet tall.
And how you told me af -

40
Gsus4
G
D
-ter it all,
we re-mem-ber to-night
43
To Coda
Em
for the rest of our lives.
(Oh.)
(Oh.)
46
Cmaj7
G
(Oh.)
(Oh.)
(Oh.)
49
D
D.S. al Coda
If these wings could fly.
Oh,
Coda
52
G

Writing's On The Wall

Words & Music by James Napier & Sam Smith

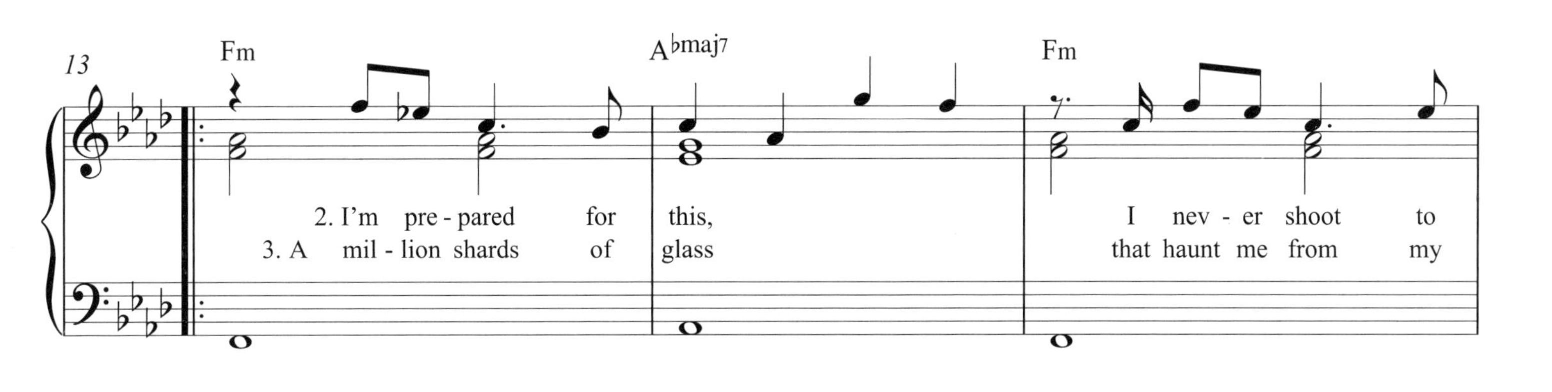
13
Fm
A♭maj7
Fm
2. I'm pre - pared for this,
3. A mil - lion shards of glass
I nev - er shoot to
that haunt me from my

16
A♭maj7
D♭
miss.
past.
But I
As the
feel like a storm is com - ing, if I'm
stars be - gin to ga - ther and the

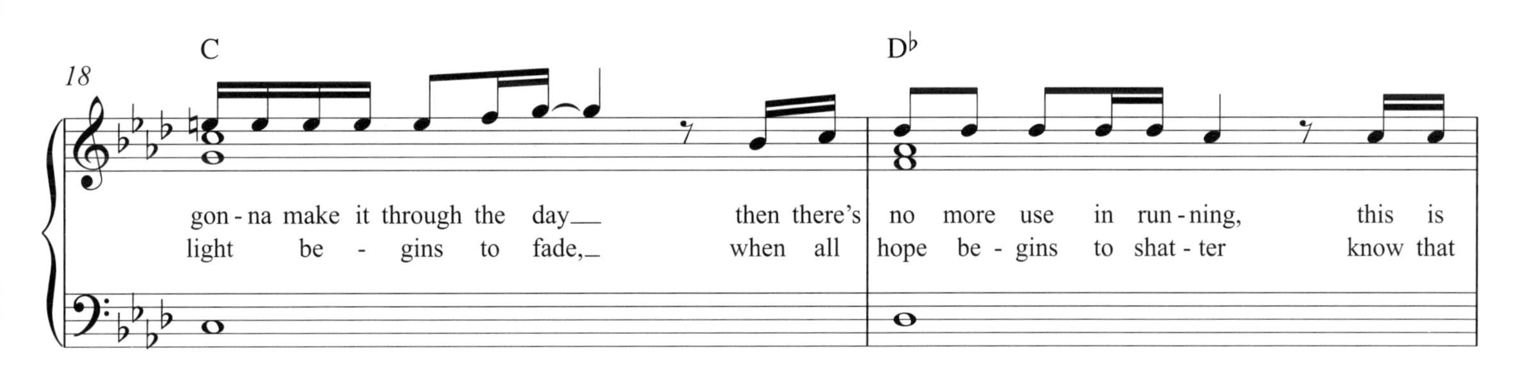
18
C
D♭
gon - na make it through the day
light be - gins to fade,
then there's
when all
no more use in run - ning, this is
hope be - gins to shat - ter know that

20
C
Fm
A♭
D♭maj7
some - thing I got - ta face.
I won't be a - fraid.
If I risk it all

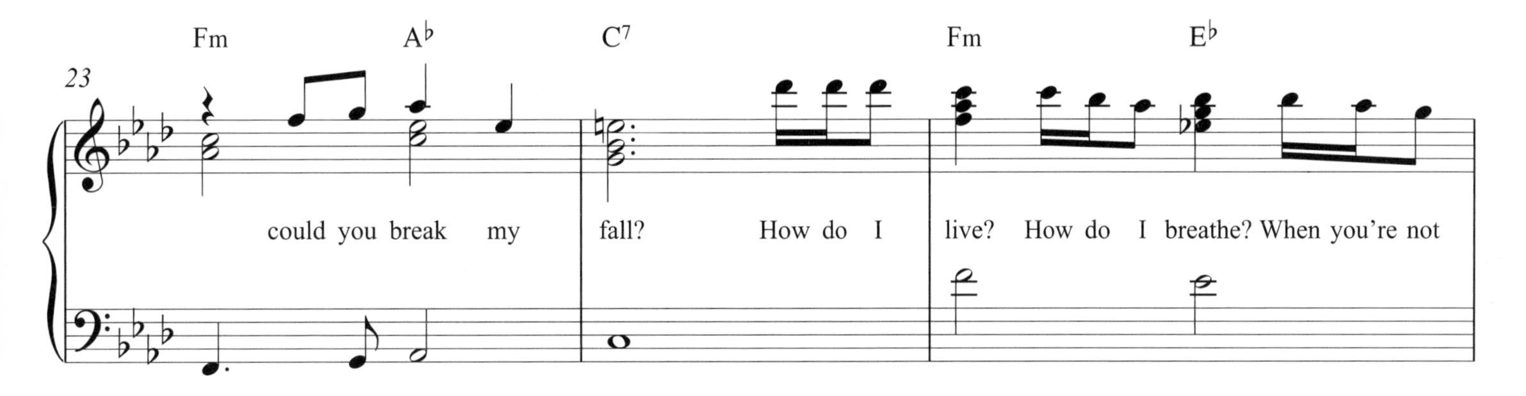
23
Fm
A♭
C7
Fm
E♭
could you break my
fall?
How do I
live? How do I breathe? When you're not

26
D♭
E♭
Fm
E♭
here I'm suf - fo - cat - ing. I want to feel
love run through my blood, tell me is

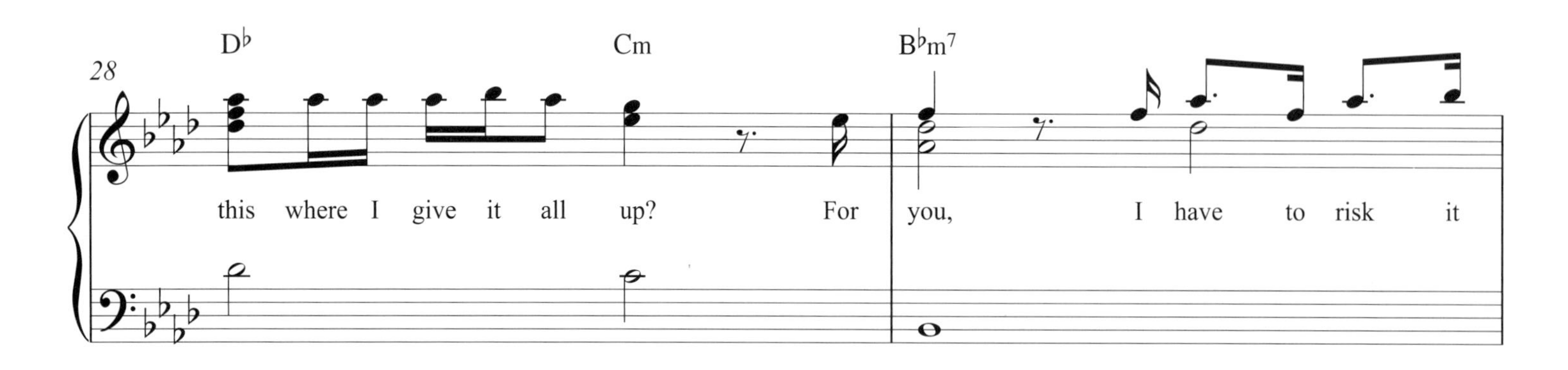
28
D♭
Cm
B♭m7
this where I give it all up? For
you, I have to risk it

30
Cm7
C7
N.C.
all
'cause the writ - ing's on the

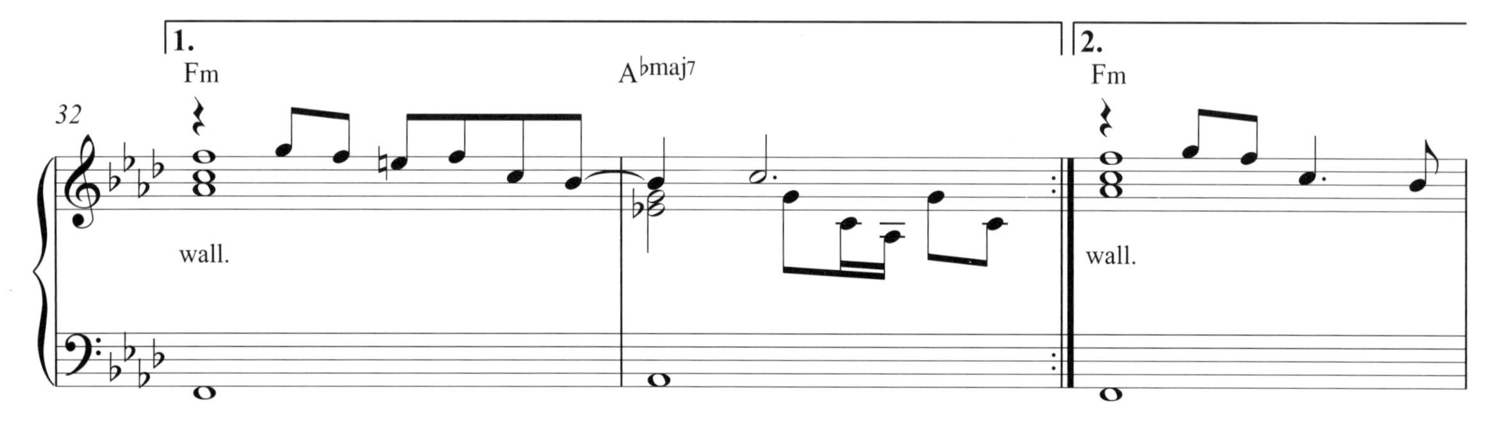
1.
2.
32
Fm
A♭maj7
Fm
wall.
wall.

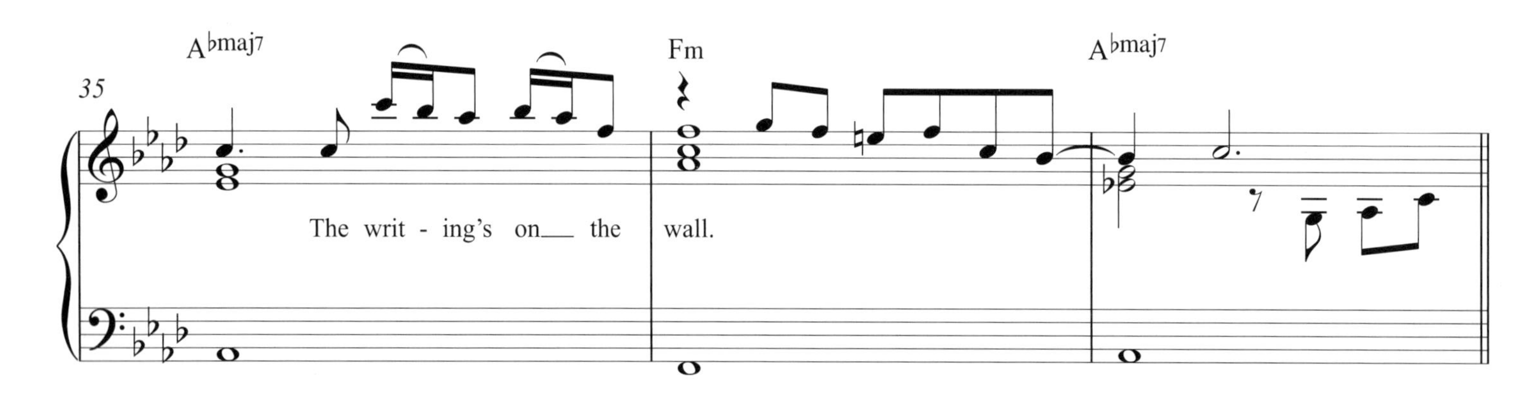
35
A♭maj7
Fm
A♭maj7
The writ - ing's on the
wall.

38
How do I
42
Fm
E♭
D♭
E♭
live? How do I breathe? When you're not here I'm suf - fo - cat - ing. I want to feel
44
Fm
E♭
1.
D♭
Cm
love run through my blood, tell me is this where I give it all up? How do I
2.
46
D♭
Cm
B♭m7
this where I give it all up? For you, I have to risk it
48
Cm7
C7
Slower
N.C.
Fm
all 'cause the writ - ing's on the wall.

1 2 3 4 5 6 7 8 9

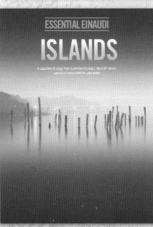

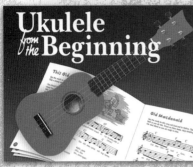

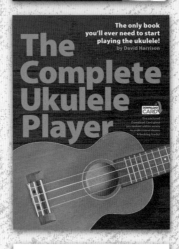

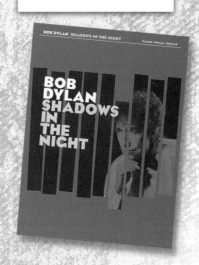